❧ MEET THE ❧
GOODPEOPLE

Wesley's Seven Ways to Share Faith

Roger Ross

Abingdon Press™
Nashville

MEET THE GOODPEOPLE:
WESLEY'S SEVEN WAYS TO SHARE FAITH

Copyright © 2015 by Abingdon Press

All rights reserved.

This book is printed on acid-free paper.

Library of Congress Cataloging-in-Publication Data

Ross, Roger, 1959- author.
  Meet the Goodpeople : Wesley's seven ways to share faith / Roger Ross.
   pages cm
  Includes bibliographical references.
  ISBN 978-1-63088-572-4 (binding: soft back : alk. paper) 1. Non church-affiliated people. 2. Evangelistic work. 3. Witness bearing (Christianity) 4. Wesley, John, 1703-1791. I. Title.
  BV4921.3.R67 2015
  269'.2—dc23

                                                        2015030749

15 16 17 18 19 20 21 22 23 24—10 9 8 7 6 5 4 3 2 1
MANUFACTURED IN THE UNITED STATES OF AMERICA

Contents

To my dad, Hugh Ross
Storyteller extraordinaire and luckiest golfer ever
Your love for people is in these pages

Acknowledgments

Hope deferred makes the heart sick,
but a dream fulfilled is a tree of life.

—Proverbs 13:12 (NLT)

A decade passed while this book sat on a shelf in my heart, deferred. It would still be there if not for a small group of people who began asking God to bring it to life more than two years ago. Thank you Tom Albin, Patty Altstetter, Mike Potts, Teresa Pratt, Barb Rudsell-Cray, and Tom Tumblin for praying with faith when there were only blank pages. Thanks, too, to our Pastors' Prayer Partners at Springfield First who have held this project in prayer for over a year.

Along the way, when self-doubt or urgent demands threatened to tank the project, God sent angels. For no apparent reason, author and editor Eddie Jones took a personal interest and made it all seem possible. Amazingly, the gracious people at Abingdon Press saw something of value and took a risk on me. Thank you Connie Stella, Kelsey Spinnato, Peggy Shearon, and Stephen Graham-Ching for your excellent guidance and stellar work.

Throughout the writing process, Patty Altstetter served as God's CEO (Chief Encouragement Officer). Thank you, Patty, for believing when things bogged down and somehow finding something positive in all 106 drafts. Thanks, too, to Cindy Arnold for her editing and formatting excellence.

God also used choruses of angels. The life-shaping impact of every faith community in my life is in this book. Thank you for showing Christ to me. I'm deeply grateful for the fantastic staff team and great people of Springfield First United Methodist Church who encouraged this work. I love putting Wesley's ways into practice with you.

Finally, special thanks to my wife, Leanne, and to my children, Zach and Jane. Day in and day out, your support, sacrifices, and love made this dream come true. Of all the angels in my life, you are the best. Now, let's get back to that board game from last year.

Introduction

They Are Everywhere

*I grew up as a child going to a church in Urbana, Illinois. My mother
was a devout Christian who wanted her children to have the same beliefs,
so I attended church every Sunday and youth group every Wednesday,
begrudgingly most of the time (I was never much of a morning person or
rule-follower).
When I became an adult, it was a relief that I didn't have to attend church
anymore, so I stopped going and pretty much ran as far away from God as
possible. That worked out for me for a time until my longing for something
more began to nag at me and I realized that I had a spiritual void in my life
that needed filled.*

—Jeannette, 41

Meet Joe and Sally Goodpeople. They pay their bills on time,
take care of their neighbor's yard, and volunteer at the Boys
and Girls Club. They have never committed a crime, don't
kick their dog, and don't know God. On the outside their lives are
filled with OK-ness. Their marriage is OK. Their work is OK. But
inside, they don't feel OK. When pushed, they admit something is
missing. There is a void at the center of their lives that won't go
away, no matter how they try to fill it. They are bright, funny, articu-
late people who have a deep-down longing to connect with something bigger than them, but they are confused about how to do it or
whether it is even possible. In their minds, church is hopelessly boring and outdated, and it is difficult to know who to trust among the

dizzying array of spiritual guides and religious options in today's market. Yet every time they hear a young child pray, they think, "I wish I could talk to God like that." Welcome to post-Christian America.

Our friends, Joe and Sally, are not alone in this new spiritual frontier. Distinguished professor of evangelism George Hunter estimates at least 180 million people in the United States are just like them, functionally non-Christian. Unlike the spiritual landscape in previous generations, the United States of America is now the largest mission field in the Western hemisphere and the third largest in the world.[1]

At the same time, curiosity about spiritual things is at peak levels in US culture. TV shows and movies about the paranormal and the coming zombie apocalypse proliferate like rabbits in the spring. Google *spirituality*, and over a quarter of a billion sites come up. The demand for values-based education, business ethics courses, and instruction on how to achieve peace of mind has never been greater. There is seemingly endless fascination with how the unseen world breaks into our everyday one.

But somehow this "spiritual awakening" has not translated into church involvement. Eighty-one percent of nonchurched adults ages twenty to twenty-nine believe that God, or a supreme being, exists, and 74 percent describe themselves as spiritual. When asked about their practice of faith, though, the most common response is, "I am spiritual, but not religious."[2] Nonchurched persons age thirty and over expressed a similar aversion to "religious" behaviors.

Here's the dilemma. How do smart, spiritually curious people who feel a void they can't fill find personal faith in Jesus Christ and a loving community to help them live a God-directed life? It's a question that has plagued me since deciding to follow Jesus my freshman year of college. Over the years, I've tried a variety of ways to encourage others to open a door to God: personal faith sharing, starting small-group Bible studies, inviting people to worship experiences—I've even drafted friends to serve the poor across the street and across the ocean. Graciously, God has used each approach to help people connect with life-changing faith. It just seemed so random. There had to be a better way, a process of some kind that would consistently produce freshly redeemed lives. Turns out, there is.

It first existed in the early church. The second chapter of Acts paints a beautiful picture of God's design for the church. In this Holy Spirit–formed community, they experienced a sense of awe, a unity, and a spirit of generosity no one had ever known. As they prayed and worshipped together in the temple courts and joyfully ate in each other's homes, God gave them favor with everyone around them. As a result, the number of love-marked lives quickly multiplied, "and the Lord added to their number daily those who were being saved."[3]

Did you notice the *d*-word in that scripture? God did not add to their number only on Sundays. It was not during special evangelistic services that people were being saved. Deep spiritual change was happening daily. Could this be God's natural design for church life? Could new people come to faith just as easily on a Tuesday as a Sunday? If so, why does that seem so unnatural now? Perhaps something is missing—something that can be found and reinstalled in the operating system of our everyday church experience. That new community in Acts 2 drew people from all walks of life into a life-changing movement of God.

Experience tells me nonchurched Goodpeople like Joe and Sally would be drawn to a movement like that too. In 1994, my wife and I moved to Champaign, Illinois, to start a new church from scratch. We had no people, no buildings, and no land (and my wife says, "no brains"), but there were three factors in our favor: (1) the prayers of hundreds of people, (2) financial support from our denomination, and (3) a white-hot vision to plant a church for people who don't go to church. Over the next thirteen years, we saw several hundred nonchurched, spiritually curious people turn their lives over to Jesus Christ and join Jesus's mission to reach the lost, the least, and the lonely of this world. In 2004, we planted a daughter church to further extend Christ's reach into the community while the mother church continued to grow to nearly eight hundred children, youth, and adults in weekly attendance. Life change toward Christ was a near-daily experience. There was a spiritual momentum that drew people to faith and sent them back to the community to serve and bless others. We could sense we were part of something larger than ourselves.

Early in this process, I stumbled onto some practices that the founder of the Methodist movement, John Wesley, used to fuel the spiritual revival in eighteenth-century England. They arose out of the challenges Wesley faced in making Christ real to both the church and the culture of his day. As a priest in the Church of England, Wesley was distraught by the powerlessness of the church to reach the vast majority of the British people. The clergy were aloof, the services were lifeless, and the poor and working class people lived their lives as if the church didn't exist. On most Sundays, only a few of society's upper crust would dot the cavernous cathedrals built to house hundreds. For all practical purposes, the church was dead.

In this dry tinder, God sparked a fire in Wesley's heart. On May 24, 1738, he reluctantly went to a prayer meeting on Aldersgate Street in London. As he listened to the speaker, suddenly his heart was "strangely warmed,"[4] and it changed him. Wesley had long been a highly committed churchman. His father, Samuel, was a priest in the Church of England, and his mother, Susanna, was a devout woman who greatly influenced her son. As a pastor's kid, Wesley knew all about how to be religious. But that night something new happened. He felt forgiven on a personal level. Like scales falling from his eyes, Wesley saw for the first time the futility of depending on his own goodness. As he described it in his journal, "I felt I did trust in Christ, Christ alone for salvation, and an assurance was given me that he had taken away my sins, even mine, and saved me from the law of sin and death."[5]

Personally experiencing the forgiving love of Christ transformed Wesley's life and ministry. He became increasingly dissatisfied with a coddled church whose primary goal was to provide religious respectability without moral transformation. God's spirit created such a holy discontent in Wesley's heart that he abandoned conventional modes of ministry and experimented with several innovative approaches. To everyone's surprise, spiritual revival broke out in England and beyond. In time, seven practices emerged as characteristic of the early Methodist movement. Here's a quick rundown of Wesley's ways to reach nonchurched people.

1. Be Devoted to Prayer

Wesley rediscovered what the church of his day had forgotten: prayer releases the power of God. He called prayer "the grand means of drawing near to God"[6] and found believing, persistent prayer to be the necessary first step to see God move. He modeled this conviction by devoting at least two hours a day to personal prayer and made fervent prayer a hallmark of the movement.

2. Go Where the People Are

When the love of Jesus Christ gripped Wesley's heart, he knew he couldn't keep it to himself. There had to be some way to reach the vast masses of people who would never darken a church door. Initially, Wesley was convinced the gospel could only be preached in the stained-glass setting of a church building. But with so few people attending church services, he was forced to consider other options. Reluctantly, Wesley began preaching in the open air. He would find a high spot on the edge of a city and speak to whoever would listen. Crowds of three, five, even ten thousand people would gather. Many of them were touched by the spirit of God and awakened to their spiritual state. A revival in England was born largely because Wesley was willing to take the gospel where the people were.

3. Speak Plain Truth

When church focuses on the theological and theoretical, most people respond with, "You lost me." In Wesley's day, the Church of England simply didn't connect with the real lives of everyday people. Ironically, the ministry of Jesus was just the opposite. When Jesus spoke, "the common people heard him gladly."[7] Wesley longed to bridge the gap between real faith and real people. Although he was a highly educated Oxford fellow and deeply steeped in the Christian tradition, he refused to parade his scholarship. He chose to speak "plain truth for plain people."[8] He intentionally shaped his language so common people could gladly hear the gospel and respond.

4. Use the Music of the Culture

Gregorian chants in Latin and heavy German music were standard fare in church services in Wesley's day. Although the words were meaningful, the music was a complete disconnect with the common people. It didn't speak their heart language. In his travels, Wesley found that pre-Christian people connected most easily with the gospel when it came through their native culture. He encouraged his brother Charles to put gospel words to the popular tunes of the day, and it caught people's hearts. Speaking in terms people could understand was part one of cracking the cultural code; music that touched the modern day soul was part two.

5. Place Everyone in a Small Group for Spiritual Growth

As Wesley began outdoor preaching in various sites around England, he soon noticed a troubling pattern. Without intentional support and encouragement, people who had moving, even ecstatic experiences of God while he was preaching would soon fall away from their newly awakened state. To provide responsible spiritual care, Wesley would only preach in venues where spiritually awakened people could be placed in small groups or "classes." His goal was not to see people have a single encounter with God but to have them experience real, lasting life change through faith in Christ. Such transformation of heart and life happens best when people do life together with a handful of others who become a spiritual family.

6. Give the Ministry to the Laity

A team member who rides the bench and a Christian who sits in a pew share an eerie similarity—they both watch other people play. Christianity was never designed to be a spectator sport. As the early Methodist movement grew rapidly, Wesley soon took his mother's advice and allowed laypersons, both men and women, to oversee classes (small groups) and preach in the society meetings (large groups). When he released the energies of the laity, the ministry multiplied even faster.

7. Use Mass Communication to Get the Word Out

In Wesley's day, the mass communication tool was the printing press. Wesley wrote numerous sermons, treatises, tracts, and books that were distributed to a wide audience to fuel the movement. Thousands of people who never heard him speak came to know Christ and grow in Christ through his writings. Of course, today the Internet and social media enable anyone with web access to have a personal platform previously unimaginable.

Why Not Now?

These seven practices, used collectively and set afire by the Holy Spirit, transformed hundreds of thousands of lives. The revival they fostered also changed the spiritual and political climate of the British Isles. Historians generally agree that the eighteenth-century evangelical revival saved England from a bloody revolution similar to others in Europe at the time. Thankfully for us, it didn't stop there. Over two centuries after Wesley's death, tens of millions of Christians around the globe can trace their spiritual roots to Wesley and the early Methodist movement. Something happened in those years that is worthy of our rapt attention. Imagine what our world could be like if a spiritual revival of that magnitude or greater were to happen in our day. Picture the number of lives transformed, marriages saved, children loved, crimes averted, and churches started or renewed. Envision the poor lifted up, prisoners liberated, races reconciled, communities restored, and nations rebuilt in the name of Jesus. The possibilities are staggering.

If you are like me, you may wonder, "If God could do that then, why not now?" Could God anoint spiritual leaders to use an updated version of these practices to change the world? It happened in Champaign. These days we're seeing it in a very different context. Since 2007, it's been my privilege to serve First United Methodist Church of Springfield, Illinois. This tall-steeple congregation was founded in 1821. Legendary frontier preacher Peter Cartwright spoke at "First Methodist" many times in its early years. Abraham Lincoln attended revival services there. Yet recently, we caught a glimpse of what God is doing now.

You heard a little of Jeannette's story at the beginning of this chapter. On a dead run from God for many years, she began attending worship with her husband. After a few months, the two of them showed up in a new member class. When a simple explanation of the gospel was given, they both responded. Since neither of them had been baptized, we arranged for their baptism on the day they joined the church. As the day grew closer, I asked if they would briefly share with the congregation their stories of newfound faith in Jesus. That Sunday, Jeannette explained how she grew up in the church, how she couldn't wait to run away from God, and how, later, she longed to fill the spiritual void in her life. But such voids aren't easily filled. At one point, she began having nightmares about eternal separation from God. She said,

> I prayed to God, asking for him to show himself to me so I could believe, but my prayers were never answered. I had finally given up my search and resolved in my mind that God really didn't exist for me, and I was okay with living in sin and going to hell. It couldn't be that bad, right?
>
> My mother passed away in 2007 from brain cancer. Since she's been gone, there have been two times she has come to me in a dream. Once, two months after she passed, to tell me that she was OK and happy. The other was in February of this year, and this last time changed my life.
>
> She had a message for me that could only have been sent by God. In my dream, I remember her standing in my living room and telling me "Be prepared, he's coming soon." I woke up knowing exactly what that message meant. I was not under God's protection, and my time was running out.
>
> Over time at my job, I have become friends with a couple from this church, and I knew they were followers in Christ. So, I told the woman about my dream and asked if I could come to church with her one Sunday. Of course, she was more than thrilled! I had never really gotten anything out of the sermons I had heard in the past but thought, "This is your last chance, what could it hurt?"
>
> Well, it didn't hurt, and as I sat listening to the sermon, I was so moved and emotionally overwhelmed. During the closing prayer, with tears running down my face, I asked God to forgive me and accepted Jesus as my savior. Since then, God has surrounded me with a great group of Christian people who have now become my sisters in faith. Instead of running from God, I am now running toward him.

When Jeannette finished her story, a hush fell over the room. We could sense the supernatural among us. After Jeannette and her husband were baptized, the entire congregation spontaneously stood and welcomed them with thunderous applause, shouts of joy, and a few tear-streaked smiles. There are days in the life of a congregation when you can feel the needle move on the transformation meter. That was one of them at our church.

Such days are meant to be the norm, not the exception. If we want to see God touch and change lives on a regular basis, we must first believe God can still do it. Only then can we put into play proven practices for producing freshly redeemed lives. The first of those practices keeps us close to the power.

Digging In

A discussion guide to help you or your group process each chapter is available at www.MeetTheGoodpeople.com as a free download. You will also find short videos with additional teaching and testimonies.

Going Global

Twenty percent of the author's royalties from this book will help provide clean water, support education, plant new churches, and fund ministry initiatives through The United Methodist Church in Liberia and other third world countries. Thank you for partnering with Christ followers around the world to transform lives.

Stay Close to the Power

God does nothing but in answer to prayer.

—John Wesley

We needed fresh power. Like many churches across the American Great Plains, the congregation had quietly lost its way. They still enjoyed each other and were able to meet their budget, but each year they grew a little smaller and a little older. You could feel the life ebbing away. As their new pastor, I was charged with turning the tide, but whatever we tried had little effect. There was a strong yet subtle resistance to any kind of spiritual change.

Slowly it dawned on me that the church needed a demonstration of God's power. They needed one of their own to accept Christ. This was no small request. Word in the pews had it that no one had seen an adult conversion in that church in fifteen years. Apparently, the last time a life was spiritually transformed, it ruffled some feathers and a concerted effort arose to return things to "normal."

At the time we were planning a retreat weekend for women. In my devotions, I kept running across passages like Psalm 63:5-6, where David prays, "My mouth praises you with joyful lips when I think of you on my bed, and meditate on you in the watches of the night."

Convicted by the Spirit, for two weeks I set the alarm for 3 a.m., got up, and prayed for that weekend. I prayed for each person on the retreat by name and asked God to break through our spiritual barrenness so someone from our church would receive Christ. Of course, I didn't tell anyone about my new night life, but I began to

1

see the spiritual temperature in the church rise. Some of the women going on the retreat decided to pray and fast for a day leading up to the weekend. They had never done that before. While in prayer, one woman saw in her mind's eye a person on the retreat receive Christ for the first time.

Anticipation was at a fever pitch when the retreat began Friday night. By Sunday afternoon, the woman that had been "seen" in prayer stood up at her table group and said, "I have struggled with this for over a year, but today, I have finally decided to accept Jesus Christ as my savior." You could have heard a tear drop. Many did. That single changed life broke the spiritual dam in that small, rural church. In the next three years, more than two dozen people came to Christ, all because a few people fervently asked God to do a new work of grace.

Prayer releases the power of God. When God's power is released, it brings spiritual increase. Whenever God wants to do a new work, God first sets people apart to pray. Prayer is the precursor to change.

Ironically, church and change don't mix well. You may remember the song "Que Sera, Sera." It was made popular as the theme song for the old *Doris Day Show* in the late 1960s. It's Spanish for "whatever will be, will be." While watching TV as a young child, the lyrics were branded into my brain before I had any idea what they meant. The song defines stoicism, a popular philosophy dating back to the Roman Empire. In essence, it claims we live in a closed universe. The outcome of things has already been determined. We are just playing out a script that was written long ago. Our only choice is to resign ourselves to our predetermined plight. Whatever will be, will be. It cannot change.

Of course, this philosophy is the direct opposite of biblical faith. Think how the ministry of Jesus would have been different if he had listened to stoic wisdom.

"The man on the mat is paralyzed, Jesus. There is nothing you can do."

"Lord, they are lepers. You can't help them. Don't go there."

"Lazarus is dead, Jesus. You're too late."

Thankfully, Jesus didn't listen to dreamless doomsayers. He knew a God who can and does change our present reality in answer to prayer. One of the single greatest motivations to pray is that everything changes, and the outcome has not been determined yet.

Chances are you're reading this because you want to see God do a new work in your life, in the lives of people you love, and in the life of your church. If so, you have a bigger role in the future than you may realize. When explaining the part he and Apollos played in starting the church in Corinth, the Apostle Paul said, "We are God's coworkers" (1 Cor 3:9 CEB). In other words, available to us is the indescribable privilege of working with God to determine the outcome of events. Nothing is set. Our prayers can change the course of human history. The future of your life, your family, your church, your community, your nation, and the world has not been written yet. There are no prepublished history books. It's all open.

Since everything changes, the only question is, "How will it change—in what direction and to what degree?" Our prayers influence those changes. Open-universe prayer is what fueled the Methodist revival in England throughout the eighteenth century. During his most productive years, John Wesley devoted at least two hours a day to personal prayer and made fervent prayer a defining characteristic of the movement. He was convinced in both his mind and his experience that believing, persistent prayer is the necessary first step to see God move. Today, over two centuries later, the group of historically related denominations that derive their inspiration from the life and teachings of John Wesley claims over eighty million adherents in 133 countries around the globe.[1]

Clearly, prayer changes things. But how?

When God's people pray, it produces a heart transplant. Praying moves us closer to the heart of God, a heart filled with compassion for people who are far from God and in deep need. Over time, a heart concerned only about ourselves is replaced with a heart that breaks for God's wandering children. God speaks about this transplant through the prophet Ezekiel in the Bible: "I will give you a new heart and put a new spirit in you; I will remove from you your heart of stone and give you a heart of flesh."[2]

This new heart is tenderized to the plight of those who have lost their way, whether they are trying to "find themselves" through destructive self-centeredness or prove their goodness by following a set of moralistic rules. As that heart of flesh begins pumping God's compassion through our veins, it produces three identifiable behaviors.

3

Chapter One

See with New Eyes

Adam Hamilton, senior pastor of The United Methodist Church of the Resurrection, spoke of a conversation he had with a woman who was a prostitute. She was older. She had been doing this kind of work a long time, and it had taken a toll on her body. You could see it in her skin.

When she was out on the street, she noticed that people would not look at her—they would look past her. She began to feel like she was invisible. One day she was out looking for johns, but "it was as if people couldn't see me," she said.

Suddenly, a younger woman from the Church of the Resurrection came up to her and cheerfully asked, "How are you today?"

She couldn't believe it. "She saw me!" the older woman said.

That began a relationship. Over time, this woman who had given away her body so many times decided to give her life to Christ. She is now in a ministry to help other women come out of that life—all because somebody saw her.[3]

Is there anyone in your life right now you are looking past? It often takes some time for our new eyes to come into focus. One night I went out to eat with Mike, a friend of mine who was far from God, and a couple who were relatively new Christians. Before arriving at the restaurant, I told the couple of my previous attempts to share Christ with Mike. Since he was pretty skittish about the Christianity thing, I thought it might help if he met other Christians that were "regular" people.

We had a great time that night. We talked about all kinds of things, laughed to the point of tears, and shared some of our life stories with each other. When it was all over, we dropped off Mike, and the three of us were in the car driving home. As we rehashed the evening, we talked about what a great guy Mike is, how funny he is, and how much he cares about his work.

Suddenly, the woman turned around and said in a completely different tone, "Roger, what's going to happen to Mike?" I knew immediately what she meant. "What is going to happen to him eternally?" For the first time in her life, she got it. She saw a person through God's eyes. Mike wasn't just a nice guy who was good for a few laughs. He had a soul. He mattered to God. Yet by his own admission, he was clueless about a relationship with Christ.

4

I said, "I don't know what's going to happen to Mike. There is still time. But unless God can use someone to get through to him, I hate to think about what might happen to him. I really do."

As Paul was going through his conversion experience in the book of Acts, something like scales fell from his eyes, and he was able to see the world through God's eyes for the first time. Those scales have to fall away from our eyes, too, to see the people in our lives the way God does.

Think with Fresh Imagination

For the last year, I have been in a small group with a couple of other guys. We meet for an hour every week to pray, discuss scripture, and ask each other a set of questions to help us grow in our faith. One of those questions is, "Have you daily prayed by name for lost people in your life to come to know Jesus Christ?"

As I prayed over and over for people in my circle of influence, God began to whisper to me, "What are you actually doing to share your faith?" This was an unsettling question, mostly because the answer was "nothing." I would talk with them as we watched our kids' ballgames, we would go out to eat occasionally, but the subject of faith and spiritual things rarely came up. For a long time, I considered inviting them to a small group like the one I enjoyed so much. But deep down, I knew that wouldn't work. My group was designed for believers who desired to grow deeper as followers of Christ. That's not where my friends were spiritually. They might come once or twice to a group like that, but they wouldn't stick. It didn't meet them at their point of spiritual need. They had doubts and questions and some wounds from the past. They needed a safe place to talk those things through. I just didn't know what that would look like.

One night I took a long car trip to my mom's house, alone. Instead of flipping on the radio or pushing in a CD, I decided to spend the time in silence listening to God. For the first hour, nothing much happened—which was good. I needed to quietly soak in God's presence. Somewhere in that second hour, God's answer to my long-time frustration burst in my mind like fireworks on the Fourth of July. It was so simple. "Start a group for people who have doubts and questions about God, faith, and life."

What my friends need is an entry-level group. Instead of having multiple individual conversations (which seldom happen due to time constraints), a group approach would serve them better on several levels. First, it is far less scary to join a group than have one-on-one meetings with "the pastor." Second, it provides a safe place to explore issues on a regular basis that are usually pushed below the surface and never discussed. Third, it shows group members that questions and doubts are normal, and they are not wrong for having them. Doubt is the leading edge of faith. It is the process by which all of us come to faith.

The longer I drove into the night, the more God revealed to me. There needed to be clear, low-level requirements to be a part of this group, such as, "Admit you don't have everything figured out." We needed some simple ground rules like this one: "Listen to one another and respect each other's opinions." We also needed some ideas about what to do during the group meetings, like icebreakers and open-ended questions to get people started. All these things were coming to me so quickly, I grabbed the only piece of paper next to me, found a stretch of interstate with no one on it, and started writing as fast as I could. As I wrote, names of people to invite flew into my head. By the time I arrived at my mom's house, the whole plan was scribbled out in detail.

I didn't know God was going to reveal those things on that long car ride. By sheer grace, I was quiet just long enough for God's gentle whisper to get through all the noise in my life. That's how God rolls. When we quiet ourselves before God, God transplants his heart of compassion for our stony one. We not only receive new eyes to see people in a spiritual light, our minds are also ignited with bursts of creativity. Kenda Creasy Dean calls it "missional imagination."[4] The Holy Spirit inspires us with innovative ways to share the love of Christ with pre-Christian people that matter so much to God. One friend has not only reclaimed his faith in Christ through one of these groups; he's now wrestling with God about becoming a pastor.

Act with Surprising Boldness

Boldness in faith doesn't come naturally to most people. One day a very dignified pastor was visiting a lady in a nursing home who was confined to a wheel chair. As he stood to leave, the lady asked him to have a word of prayer. He gently took her hand and prayed that God would be with her to bring her comfort, strength, and healing. When he finished praying her face began to glow. She said softly, "Pastor, would you help me to my feet?"

Not knowing what else to do, he helped her up. At first, she took a few uncertain steps. Then she began to jump up and down, then to dance and shout and cry with happiness until the whole nursing home was up for grabs. After she was quieted, the solemn pastor hurried out to his car, closed the door, grabbed hold of the steering wheel, and prayed a little prayer, "Lord, don't you EVER do that to me again!"[5]

Jesus makes some outrageous promises about prayer.

"Ask and it will be given to you; seek and you will find; knock and the door will be opened to you."[6]

"If you abide in me, and my words abide in you, ask for whatever you wish, and it will be done for you."[7]

If we took Jesus at his word, nothing could keep us from praying. When hit with a problem or concerned about someone's eternal destiny, it would be the first thing we do. But for most Christians and churches, prayer can be the last thing we do, when everything else hasn't worked. What keeps God's people from naturally going to prayer as the primary means to effect change?

To be honest, we like our predictable routines. They are safe and familiar. They create a comfort zone of religious respectability without the turbulence of moral transformation. Prayer messes that up. If we sincerely pray, we won't stay the same. We won't see people the same way or think the same thoughts. As Richard Foster puts it, "To pray is to change. Prayer is the central avenue God uses to transform us. If we are unwilling to change, we will abandon prayer as a noticeable characteristic of our lives"[8]

At some level, we know prayer is subversive to the status quo. God is neither predictable nor tame. To call on God's name could turn everything upside down. That's why prayer is not for the faint of heart. Praying unleashes a power that brings change, emboldens our spirit, and launches us into uncharted territory.

One Saturday morning at a men's retreat, a simple explanation of the gospel was offered. During an "open mic" time that followed, a guy stepped up and said, "My name is Geno, and I accepted Jesus Christ as my savior today." Every man in the place stood, clapped, and cheered. It was exhilarating.

Geno proceeded to share his story. He had just retired the previous spring from teaching at Cambridge High School for thirty-three years. He's well-known in that county-seat town of 2,200 people in northwest Illinois. He went on to speak very vulnerably about difficult things he had experienced in life and what the love of Christ meant to him. When he was finished, the group prayed for him and gave him a second standing ovation for sharing so boldly.

In the room that day was David Joyce, pastor of the Cambridge United Methodist Church where Geno has been a member for decades. When Dave heard Geno's story, he asked Geno to share it with the church on Sunday morning.

Geno was hesitant. He didn't want to take time away from Dave's message. Dave said, "Geno, I don't care if I preach at all tomorrow. What you have to say is more important." Reluctantly, he accepted the invitation.

When Geno shared his story on Sunday, he spoke for thirty minutes. There wasn't a dry eye in the place. When he finished, Geno asked everybody to come forward, join hands, and he led them in a prayer.

No one can remember anything like that ever happening at the Cambridge United Methodist Church. When a friend called on Sunday afternoon to describe what took place, I nearly dropped the phone. That's my home church! I came to Christ in that church. Those were the people who prayed for me and affirmed my call to ministry. But that church had fallen on hard times. In fact, just two years before, it looked like the church wouldn't make it. Worship attendance had dropped from 140 to less than 60 in seven years—and there was no bottom in sight. There were no youth. They had no Sunday school classes for kids. No one ever used the nursery. Day by day, the light was growing dimmer.

When all seemed lost, God called someone to pray. Concerned about the future, Jeane Downing decided something should be done for the National Day of Prayer. She offered to show up at the church at 10 a.m. that first Thursday in May. If anyone wanted to pray, they could come.

Apparently, word got out and twelve people from four churches in town showed up. After Jeane read a couple of appropriate things, she sat down on the front pew and started to tear up. She said, "I am so worried that our church is dying." Immediately, everyone else chimed in. They had the same fears. None of the churches were do-

8

ing well. It got to be noon, and they decided they needed to meet again. They set a time for the following Thursday at ten.

They have been meeting every Thursday since. Want to know what is happening? Jeane says, "We're seeing tumors shrink, people sell houses and get jobs, and people cured of cancer. We anointed one man and prayed for him before his heart surgery. When he was in the hospital, completely prepped for surgery, they took him for a final EKG, and the doctor said he'd improved so much he didn't need it! We've prayed for our pastor and our church and the Lord has really blessed us!"

That's an understatement. The church has more than tripled in attendance. They have a Sunday school for kids again. They prayed for a youth group and in less than one year, they had twenty kids coming!

How could this happen? Jeane doesn't have any special qualifications. She's never been to seminary. She just decided to get together with a few other people and pray. That was her only strategy. The founder of the Methodist movement understood how this happens. John Wesley said, "God does nothing but in answer to prayer; and even they who have been converted to God without praying for it themselves (which is exceeding rare) were not without the prayers of others. Every new victory which a soul gains is the effect of a new prayer."[9]

Wesley knew that someone had to "pray the price." They are having spiritual revival at Cambridge United Methodist Church because Jeane and her prayer group are praying it into existence. Given the spiritual condition of that church and community over the last three decades, it's no exaggeration to say, "If it can happen in Cambridge, it can happen anywhere."

In the New Testament, James, the brother of Jesus, says, "You do not have because you do not ask God."[10]

If you want your church to come alive and reach nonchurched people with the good news of Jesus Christ, you must help people discover how to personally seek God. Here are four practical ways to release the power of God in your congregation and beyond.

Preach on Prayer

When surveyed, about 70 percent of Americans say they pray weekly. But for most people, prayer is a spiritual slot machine in the sky with a big ear attached to it. If they pour in just the right words, the screen will come up all cherries, a bell will go off, and their answer will slide into their lives. It's more about hitting the jackpot than striking up a conversation with God.

To help people understand the true relationship they are meant to have with the Lover of their souls, pastors must make prayer part of the regular preaching menu. Most people would love to have a more intimate relationship with God, if they only knew how. Consider preaching a four-part series to help people get started. I've used a simple series called "Talking to God." Over a four-week span, I addressed basic questions most people have: Does praying change anything? Where do I start? Does God ever talk back? What about unanswered prayers?

The response to this series has always been positive, because it touches a deep hunger in all of us. I have later followed it up with various series and individual messages such as "Pray Where U R," "Unfiltered Prayers," "The Model Prayer," and "Unnoticed Prayer." It's our practice to preach at least one series a year on prayer. In some ways, it is like the topic of stewardship. It must be revisited regularly. If we don't keep pushing prayer to the front burner, it inevitably falls off the back one. Once that happens, it no longer has a transforming effect on the congregation or our outreach. Instead, we resort to doing ministry on our own power, and nothing of eternal value is accomplished.

Preaching sets the bar for the church, but to internalize the message there must also be a teaching component.

Teach People How to Pray

I confess. For a long time, I thought some people were just born prayers. Somewhere along the line God zapped them with the ability to pray. Some people got it and some people didn't. Unfortunately, I didn't.

Imagine my surprise when I discovered I was wrong. A friend had recommended Richard Foster's book, *Celebration of Discipline.* As I read the chapter on prayer, the light came on. For the first time, I realized prayer was not *hocus pocus.* There was a form and order to it. It wasn't dependent on getting the words right or catching God on a good day. It was much firmer than that. There were principles I could learn and practices I could embrace. My relationship with God has never been the same.

When we take time to teach people how to pray through classes, small groups, and mentoring relationships, the light comes on for them as well. They discover the same truth—that prayer is learnable. It is a spiritual skill anyone can pick up. No prior knowledge or talent is necessary. All it takes is a desire to know God and a willingness to experiment in the laboratory of prayer called everyday life. This is great news since most people readily admit they don't know how prayer works, have never been taught basic kinds of prayer (simple, meditative, intercessory, the examen, confession, and so on), and don't know how to establish essential practices for living prayer.

For the last several years, we've taken aim at this issue by offering a "Teach Us to Pray" class for four to six weeks beginning in January. It's co-led by pastors and a layperson, and we present new material each time. Surprisingly, it's more popular each year. The first time we held the class, we asked people why they signed up. One woman in the back said, "I've been going to this church for over forty years, and no one has ever taught me how to pray." Our hope is that she and many others are now enjoying a personal walk with God that is deep and life giving.

We have also found that all-church studies during Lent can significantly help people connect with God. We use a book and DVD series like *The Power of a Whisper* by Bill Hybels or Martha Grace Reese's *Unbinding Your Heart*, which provides excellent daily prayer exercises. Each weekend, we focus our preaching and worship experiences on the topic that will be discussed in the Sunday school classes and small groups that week. These seasons create a baseline of prayer knowledge and a common vocabulary to share our experiences with God.

When prayer is established as a priority and people are taught how to pray, we can then harness that power for kingdom purposes.

Mobilize People to Pray

One day a pastor and a bus driver went to heaven. The bus driver got a big, beautiful mansion with large rooms. The pastor got a small, one-room bungalow. The pastor went to St. Peter and said, "How come I got such a dinky place and that bus driver got a beautiful mansion? I've preached the gospel all my life."

11

St. Peter said, "Well, when you preached, people fell asleep. But when that bus driver drove, people prayed."

That's one way to mobilize people to pray. Here are three other options.

Create a Prayer Leadership Team

Churches are known for organizing every ministry under the sun. We have education councils, personnel committees, trustees, finance committees, usher and greeter teams, choirs, worship teams, evangelism committees, missions councils, student ministry teams, and on and on. We are organized to the hilt, except when it comes to prayer.

Why not find some of your best pray-ers and ask them to form a prayer leadership team? It would be their responsibility to lift up the value of prayer in the congregation, set prayer goals, and mobilize people to pray. Recently, our prayer leadership team set a goal of a thousand hours of prayer during Lent. They determined if one hundred people prayed for fifteen minutes a day for forty days, it would add up to a thousand hours. They cast the vision, encouraged people to sign up, and gave those who registered specific prayer points to focus on each week. In the end, we had 103 people participate, and we exceeded our thousand-hour goal. Some might wonder what practical good comes out of such an exercise. In our case, quite a lot. Ten days after exceeding our goal, our church's former building that had been on the market for over seven years suddenly sold.

An old axiom says, "What gets measured, gets done." The opposite is also true. "What doesn't get measured, doesn't happen." If you want to see the power of God released, create a team whose sole responsibility is to mobilize people to pray.

Calendar Prayer

When do people in your church gather each week to pray? This does not include the perfunctory prayer before and after committee meetings. "Lord, help us get through this agenda quickly tonight, so we can go home and watch the game." Is there a time on the church calendar every week where people come together with no other agenda than to pray? If not, it's easy to default to a nice organization run primarily on well-meaning human effort. Jesus said, "Apart from me you can do nothing"[1] For years, this verse made no sense to me. I knew by sheer effort, I could do a lot. In fact, some coworkers nicknamed me "The Tornado" because every time I showed up there would be a whirlwind of activity. It took me a while to understand what Jesus was really saying: "Apart from me, you can do nothing *of eternal value*." Lots of activity. Nothing that lasts.

When we value something we allot time for it. Every week we have worship services, music rehearsals, staff meetings, Bible studies, youth groups, and a lot more, because we calendar them. Talk with your newly created prayer leadership team and pick the best time and the best place to pray. When we set a weekly time to honor God with our prayers, we invite God to do the things we cannot. Things that last.

Create a Church-Wide Prayer Team

Our world is all about mobile. Several years ago, laptops started outselling desktops. More recently, tablets started outselling laptops. Now, cell phones are getting larger, so they can be an all-in-one "phablet." People want the freedom to connect anywhere at any time.

Of course, that's always been the case with God. Prayer is a 24/7 all-access activity. The challenge is to focus those prayers for maximum impact. When light is diffused, it scatters throughout the room. But when it is focused, it becomes a laser that can cut through steel.

The best way I've found to help a large number of people be mobile and laser-focused is through our church-wide prayer team. This team has no meetings. Instead, team members make this simple commitment: I will remember our church, its staff, and its ministries to the Lord for a few moments each day.

As for my part, I send an update to all prayer team members at the beginning of the month that provides a brief teaching on prayer, recaps how God has been answering our prayers, and offers prayer focus points for the next month. When we first started the prayer team at Springfield First, my hope was to have two hundred people praying every day. We now have more than double that who pray at whatever time and place they choose each day. Their focused prayers are cutting through barriers and creating spiritual break-throughs.·

Once we have mobilized people through a prayer leadership team, a calendared prayer time, and a focused means to pray on the go, there is only one thing left to do.

Pray!

To paraphrase Wesley, "Nothing happens until somebody starts praying." Our personal desire to seek God sets the tone for those around us. But setting aside a regular time and a regular place to meet with God each day is no easy challenge. It must be fought for repeatedly. Whether you're a church leader or a health-care provider, in the marketplace or law enforcement, a teacher or student, a mechanic or stay-at-home parent, life is filled with many demands. There is always one more person to see, one more phone call to make, ten more e-mails to send, and a big, hairy issue that refuses to be resolved. Our work is never done. Sometimes it's so consuming, we get lost in it.

A while back I noticed a disturbing trend. During a particularly crazy two-month period, I had missed more days of writing in my journal than I had missed in the last five years combined. Something was wrong. I was out of alignment. When I called my spiritual director, he immediately put his finger on it. "The busyness of your ministry has distracted you from the source of your ministry—namely, God."

He was dead right. His next words sank deep. "As pastors, we give too much space to the ministry in our lives. God is first, not the ministry. Hold the ministry more lightly. It is secondary. It flows from your primary relationship with God."

Ironically, the enemy of our souls can use even the ministry to tempt us to do too much good and keep us away from our truest good—our relationship with God. Unhurried time with the Lord of life is the only known antidote.

What is tempting you to abandon your time alone with God these days? Our world is full of unworthy pursuits that distract and derail us. We've all been down that road. But there are times when we get caught up in a cause that is compelling and good. It's just not our truest good.

By guarding our primary relationship with God, we receive the true gifts all our other pursuits falsely promise. In God's presence, we experience a purer, deeper, more encompassing love than this world can offer. We feel accepted for who we are and encouraged as we grow. We see the person, character, and will of God revealed on a personal level. And best of all, we hear God's whisper. In those quiet moments, God directs our path and gives us fresh courage to follow God's leading. Without these gifts, we could never make the journey.

Staying close to the power transforms us. It also transforms our relationships. This new life propels us to go places and do things we could have never imagined.

Prayer

Lord, you know where I need a new work of grace in my heart. Give me a heart transplant. Help me to set aside time alone with you to hear your voice and follow your leading for my life.

Hiding God's Word in My Heart

I will give you a new heart and put a new spirit in you; I will remove from you your heart of stone and give you a heart of flesh.

—Ezekiel 36:26 (NIV)

Discussion guide available at www.MeetTheGoodpeople.com.

On the Go

To reach people that no one is reaching you have to do things
that no one is doing.

—Craig Groeschel

I t's our unofficial midwinter holiday. In early February each year, Americans drop everything and huddle around a screen to watch grown men intentionally run into each other for four hours. It's the Super Bowl, and it's the hottest ticket of the year. If you haven't bought yours yet, start saving now. For a recent Super Bowl, the average price on NFL Ticket Exchange was $4,131.[1] That's per ticket. You'll probably want four.

But if that is a little steep, you can grab a great seat for a fraction of the cost. Recently, just for the big game, over 9 million TVs were purchased.[2] As we sat down in front of our big screens, Americans consumed 1.25 billion chicken wings. Had they been laid end-to-end, they would have circled the circumference of the Earth more than twice. For those with the munchies, nearly 46 million pounds of chips were sold just before game time. Of course, we needed dip with that, so add 71 million pounds of avocados. That's enough guacamole to fill Lucas Oil Stadium in Indianapolis, where the big game has been played.[3] Not surprisingly, antacid sales on the Monday after the game go up 20 percent.[4]

But it's worth it. Each year we tune into the biggest American sports spectacle of the year. Over 114 million people watched a recent Super Bowl, the largest American TV audience ever. That compared with 32 million who watched the president's State of the Union a couple of weeks before.[5]

As you can imagine, the National Football League couldn't be happier. The NFL is making more money than ever. They easily outdistance Major League Baseball as the most successful professional sport in America. Of course, that means they can charge more. In 1967, the first televised Super Bowl charged $42,000 for a thirty-second commercial. In 2015, the take was $4.5 million for thirty seconds, up $500,000 from 2014.[6]

You may wonder, "What are they doing with all that money?" They're expanding their reach. The Super Bowl is beamed to around 200 countries and broadcast in 25 languages.[7] It stopped being a purely American affair decades ago. That's why the NFL now plays three regular season games in London each fall and proposes to make it four in the near future. To increase their exposure at home, the NFL recently added five more Thursday night games, so all thirty-two teams will play in prime time at least once. They have also released a Spanish language NFL Red Zone channel.

Make no mistake about it. The NFL is trying to reach the world. They are spending billions of dollars and employing every creative idea they can imagine to make more football fans.

But they are not the first to want to reach the world. Some time ago, God looked at the world he created and saw it was marred by sin—a selfish disregard for God. To bring humanity back into a loving relationship, God chose a people to be his very own, a light to the nations. They were to be God's instrument to bring salvation to the entire world. Through these people, God performed miracles to demonstrate his power and gave them signs to show his presence, but still many of God's own rebelled. Time and again, God sent prophets to call the people back, priests to minister to the people, and kings to lead the people. Although these creative approaches worked for a while, eventually the people turned away again.

When all seemed lost, God deployed a bold, risky, never-been-tried idea to reach every person on the planet. Jesus describes it this way. "For God so loved the world that he gave his only Son, so that everyone who believes in him may not perish but may have eternal life."[8]

God must have thought, "If they won't listen to the people I send, I will go there myself. Through my Son, I will take on human flesh. I'll breathe their air. I'll eat their food. I'll walk their streets. I'll become one of them. Then they will understand my love for them."

All this was for a special purpose revealed in the next verse. "Indeed, God did not send the Son into the world to condemn the world, but in order that the world might be saved through him."[9]

God is on a mission. Contrary to what some believe, it is not to condemn people, but to save the entire world through the sacrificial love of his Son. What motivates this mission? Love. Love for children that are hurting, alone, and adrift in life. That's what drove God to think in crazy new ways. Chances are you would do the same.

If someone said, "You must give me $20,000 by Wednesday," you would probably say, "I can't do that. I don't have that kind of money laying around. It's just not possible." But everything would change if a doctor said, "Your daughter needs an operation by Wednesday, or she will die. It is not covered by insurance, and it will cost $20,000. Her life is in your hands."

Suddenly, you would get very creative. You would dig through your finances, talk to family and friends, or go to a bank. You would sell stuff if necessary. You would do things you had never done before to find $20,000 because you love your daughter and nothing would matter more than saving her life.

Love is a powerful motivating force. It gets us out of ourselves and thinking in ways we have never considered. It's the kind of creative approach God modeled in sending his Son. It had never been done before, and it was costly beyond measure. But entering our world in human flesh made it possible to reach the people God loved who had never been reached.

A young John Wesley was captured by this same love. The church of his day in eighteenth-century England was lifeless and irrelevant to its culture. But when the love of Jesus Christ gripped Wesley's heart, he knew he couldn't keep it to himself. There had to be some way to reach the vast masses of people who would never darken the door of a church.

This caused great conflict in Wesley's heart. As a priest of the Church of England, he thought the only appropriate place to preach was behind the stained-glass safety of a church building. But hardly anyone attended church services in those days. It didn't connect with the real lives of everyday people. To make matters worse, his warmed-heart experience of Christ's love in 1738 branded him an "enthusiast." All but a handful of his fellow clergy considered him an obnoxious fanatic, so they refused to have him preach in their churches.

In the spring of 1739, his friend George Whitefield invited Wesley to leave London and come to Bristol, a bustling port city of fifty thousand along the southwest coast of England. With church doors closed to Whitefield as well, George began preaching out of doors. The results were dramatic. When Wesley arrived on April 1, he witnessed Whitefield preaching to about thirty thousand coal miners and their families on a hillside in Kingswood, just outside Bristol.[10] The sight was both exhilarating and agonizing to Wesley. His heart longed to reach large numbers of pre-Christian people, but this new method didn't seem "proper." As he describes in his journal, he had long been "so tenacious of every point relating to decency and order that I should have thought the saving of souls *almost a sin* if it had not been done *in a church*."[11] But that was about to change.

On April 2, 1739, at age thirty-five, Wesley took the plunge:

> At four in the afternoon I submitted to 'be more vile,' and proclaimed in the highways the glad tidings of salvation, speaking from a little eminence in a ground adjoining the city, to about three thousand people.[12]

That was the tipping point of the eighteenth-century revival. If Wesley had waited for those three thousand people to come to church, he would have died standing at the altar. Instead of making them come to him, Wesley went to them.

The early days of the revival felt like a page out of the book of Acts. Compelled by the love of Christ, Wesley would head to the Kingswood coal mines at 5 a.m. dressed in his clerical garb. He'd stand on a miner's cart and preach to thousands of workers before they spent the next twelve hours down a mine shaft. As he spoke, many of them were touched by the spirit of God. Tears would cut little channels through the coal dust on the miners' cheeks. Countless times, surly men had their hearts softened by the word of God and turned toward faith. After his first month in the Bristol area, Wesley estimated his outdoor preaching drew 47,500 listeners.[13]

As people responded to his message, Wesley invited them to meet with him afterward. All that were "awakened" to their spiritual state and expressed a "desire to flee from the wrath to come" were organized into "classes" of about twelve people. We would call them small groups today. Every group had a trained leader and a specific agenda designed to help each person grow in his or her faith. I will detail how the classes fueled the revival in chapter 5. When Wesley wed outdoor preaching with small-group discipleship, the Methodist movement caught fire.

Are you willing to "be more vile"? Who are the people you know that could die before they ever darken the door of church? How will the forgiving love and leadership of Jesus Christ be extended to them?

The GO! Principle

Jesus's final charge to his disciples was to "go and make disciples of all nations."[14] To follow Jesus is to go to the "nations," the people groups in your neighborhood, school, community, and beyond that don't know him yet. It is to take the initiative. What might it look like to "be more vile" these days?

A guy in our church likes to hang out at Panera. He'll get some coffee, open his Bible at a table, and put up a card that says, "I'm available to pray, talk, or listen."

A new church in Iowa was all fired up about reaching their community. They didn't want to take people out of existing churches, so they bought shot glasses and distributed them to all the bars in town. Each glass read,

Cross Point United Methodist Church.
Give us a shot.

That got them in trouble with a few church people. (Makes you wonder how they knew.)

Craig Groeschel, senior pastor of LifeChurch.tv, one of the most missionally creative (and largest) churches in the United States, brainstormed with his team about the best advertising places to attract nonchurched people. They came up with a risky idea: place their church ad on a high-traffic porn website.[15]

Are you willing to be more vile?

Times have changed in America. In the 1950s and 1960s, it was expected that people would go to church. Those of us in church back then didn't have to do anything. We simply published the service times, opened the doors, and welcomed people in. The world came to us. But the world is not coming on its own anymore. Our time is now more like Wesley's day. We must go to them. We must creatively think of ways to meet them on their turf and their terms and show Christ's love in practical ways.

Not long ago, there was a front-page article in my local newspaper titled, "Where Bible Study Meets Beer." It was announcing a new place to worship in town—not in a church building and not on a Sunday morning. Over sixty people came out for the launch of "Bar Church" on Wednesday nights at Stella Blue in downtown Springfield. It's promoted as "a place where people can meet for worship, socialize and grab a pint at the same time—without judgment."[16]

Brandon Damm, the church's twenty-six-year-old pastor, explained it this way. "Jesus was a lover of people and went into the world. . . . That's kind of our mission with Bar Church. It's to go where the people are." Referring to Jesus, he said, "The guy I know hung out with prostitutes. The guy I know hung out with tax collectors. The guy I know hung out with people that drank."[17]

All true. Yet it hasn't made Brandon's life any easier. When Bar Church launched a Facebook page, he received some "hate mail" through the site. Some church people thought the idea promoted drunkenness. That couldn't be further from the truth. For some time he's worked with recovery and sobriety programs through the church that's sponsoring him. Brandon's just trying to meet people on their own turf and their own terms.

Although I have never been much of a bar-goer, I couldn't wait to go to Bar Church. A few days before, I put the word out to my Facebook friends and several people from our church joined me. To my surprise, I didn't feel out of place at all. In fact, it was exciting. A place that often makes people forget about God was now being used to draw people closer to God—most of whom rarely darken the door of a church building.

When I talked to Brandon after the service, he said, "People get all worked up about having worship here. It's really not about being in a bar. It's about being in a place where people feel comfortable. When they are comfortable, they are more receptive to the gospel."

Jesus was always getting in trouble for hanging out with the wrong people in the wrong places. His critics called him a glutton and a drunk. Jesus didn't just risk his reputation; he ruined it. And it didn't bother him in the least. Are you willing to be more vile?

This GO! principle applies far beyond the geographical. Many people are hurting emotionally, relationally, and financially. To meet them where they are, we must build on-ramps to a new life. After the loss of a loved one, many in our community have found healing and hope through the grief support classes our church offers. People experiencing the pain of divorce have found a life they didn't know possible through caring groups that address the changes divorce brings. On the front side of that equation, we offer a one-day marriage preparation workshop for couples that are seriously dating, engaged, or newly married to provide the tools they need to build a healthy relationship. Marriage mentors are also available to walk with new couples through a season of life. Regardless of the season, money management is a huge issue these days. The deep anxiety around having more month than money and no real plan for the future places an enormous strain on individuals and families. Both community and church members have been grateful for the freedom they've found through a biblically grounded course on personal finances.

To go to another group in our community, we must first meet them at their point of physical need. James, the brother of Jesus, said, "Imagine a brother or sister who is naked and never has enough food to eat. What if one of you said, 'Go in peace! Stay warm! Have a nice meal!'? What good is it if you don't actually give them what their body needs?"[18] A gently used clothing store, a local food pantry, assistance with the cost of prescription drugs, home repair for single moms and the elderly, shelter and meals for homeless persons, and a myriad of other possibilities provide ways to meet the physical needs of people. Showing Christ's love in physical ways opens a door to experience Christ's love on a spiritual level.

The final frontier is to go where people are spiritually. Sadly, most Christians think people who don't go to church are antichurch and don't want to hear about God or Jesus. But those perceptions don't square with reality. In a comprehensive study that surveyed over two thousand unchurched persons and personally interviewed over three hundred people from all fifty US states and Canada, Thom Rainer discovered that unchurched, pre-Christian people would in most cases welcome a caring, nonjudgmental conversation about faith and beliefs. In fact, they are waiting for those of us who follow Christ to bring it up!

Rainer says Sharon's story is not uncommon. She lives in San Diego and has two Christian coworkers at her brokerage firm. In fact, she and her two friends were among the top brokers in Southern California.

> "Mike and Jenny [her coworkers] and I make more money than any of us ever dreamed. But we've all talked about how the money hasn't really made us happier. I know that they go to church regularly, so I sometimes hint to see if they'll say anything about it," she told [interviewers].
>
> "One time we got into this real serious discussion about the important things in life," Sharon continued. "I decided just to ask them outright if church was that important to them. You should've seen how red their faces turned. They said a few things like, 'Of course it is,' but you could tell they weren't comfortable at all talking about religious issues. I just can't understand it. I think I'm really searching for something, but no one seems to want to talk to me."[19]

Do you know anyone like Sharon? Spirituality is one of the hottest topics in our culture. There are people in your life and mine who would love to talk about God and faith and church—if we'll just start the conversation. In fact, Rainer and his research team were amazed by the level of spiritual openness they found. In their surveys and interviews, 82 percent of pre-Christian people said they would be "very likely" or "somewhat likely" to attend church if they were invited by someone they trusted. Of course, this doesn't mean they will come the first time you ask, but if you build a trusting relationship with someone over time, eight out of ten pre-Christian people who do not currently attend church anywhere are likely to come.

Even more fascinating are the five stages of faith Rainer and his team discovered among unchurched people. It turns out our pre-Christian friends, neighbors, and coworkers are not on a one-size-fits-all spiritual journey. There are different levels of responsiveness that can be seen in your golfing buddy, your sister-in-law, or your childhood friend. Each one is tagged *U* for "Unchurched."

U5: Highly antagonistic and even hostile to the gospel

While many Christians cower from sharing their faith for fear of running into someone like this, U5s make up only 5 percent of the unchurched in America.

U4: Resistant to the gospel, but with no antagonistic attitude

23

U4s are 21 percent of the unchurched population. Unlike U5s, they are open to special presentations of the gospel at Christmas or Easter, but they are unlikely to respond immediately. They need time to become more receptive.

U3: Neutral, with no clear signs of being interested yet perhaps being open to discussion

U3s are the single largest group, comprising 36 percent of the 160 million unchurched people in America, by Rainer's count. The 57 million U3s are characterized more by what they are not. They are neither resistant nor receptive to the gospel.

U2: Receptive to the gospel and church

U2s are the second largest group, with 43 million unchurched. They know something is missing in their lives. They are spiritually seeking and would be very interested in an invitation to church.

U1: Highly receptive to hearing and believing the good news

Rainer estimates there are 17 million U1s in America. Their overwhelming reason for not attending church is "busyness." They regularly pray, hold many Christian beliefs, and are simply waiting for someone to share the hope available in Christ. They are truly the low-hanging fruit.[20]

Clearly, the unchurched are a diverse group. Understanding their spiritual condition will help us meet them where they are, so we can encourage them to take the next step on their journey toward Christ. But don't miss this staggering statistic. By Rainer's count, 60 million unchurched, pre-Christian people are receptive or highly receptive to receiving the good news of Jesus and joining his mission in this world. Another 57 million are neutral and open to discussion. Jesus's words to his disciples have never been more true: "The size of the harvest is bigger than you can imagine, but there are few workers."[21]

Ironically, modern day disciples tend to think the harvest is puny. "No one is really interested in God or spiritual things these days." But Jesus sees things through God's eyes. He sees a mind-blowing number of people ripe for the gospel. To him, it's a labor issue. A farmer told me one day, "When my crop is ripe, there are hundred things that could happen to it, and all of them are bad. I've got to get that crop out of the field as quickly as possible." Jesus, the master grower, sees it the same way. What's his solution? "Therefore, plead with the Lord of the harvest to send out workers for his harvest."[22]

Finding Your Why

For Jesus, the labor issue is really a prayer issue. "Plead with the Lord," he says. To create a worker for the harvest, something has to happen in a person's heart. A new *why* must form. It goes something like this:

> I thought I was here to please myself. My goal was to find happiness and success, and to live a comfortable, stress-free life doing whatever I wanted. But my own pride and selfishness derailed that dream and left me in a pit of emptiness and despair. When I invited Christ into my life, I hoped he would make my life infinitely better by forgiving my sins and mistakes, giving me peace of mind, and helping me find the happiness and success I'd always longed for. And he did, at first.
>
> But he didn't leave it there. The longer I walked with Jesus, the more I began to see that life is not about me. It's not about my happiness or success. It's about discovering God's will for my life and living it out with uncommon courage. Often this means doing things that stretch me way out of my comfort zone and going places that never show up in a resort catalogue. It's ruined my golf game and dramatically affected my net worth. But I've never been more myself than I am now. Jesus's deep love for me has changed the composition of my heart and given me a love for the people he loves, those who are still far from him and in deep need.

When we plead with the Lord for workers, God forms a new purpose in our hearts, one that aligns with Jesus's purpose. Jesus had a really clear sense of why.

"For the Son of Man came to seek and save those who are lost."[23] Jesus was always on a mission. You see it from the first invitation He makes to his would-be disciples: "Follow me, and I will make you fish for people."[24] His purpose was crystal clear. When I became a follower of Jesus, something of that mission got in me too.

I grew up in the church. Sadly, the church of my youth was going through a pretty dry season in its life. Although God has turned that around now, years ago most people would have said our church was boring, passionless, and spiritually dead. Even still, there was a remnant of life. God used people there, primarily my Sunday school teachers, to lead me to faith in Jesus.

But many of my friends who also had spiritual questions and were also seeking the truth couldn't relate to the church of my youth. They hadn't grown up in the system and had no connection with the rich traditions of the past or the jargon of church people. They didn't know how to break into the social circles and didn't have the patience to wait five or ten years before they could say or do something. It just didn't work for them. Instead, they wrote the church off and unknowingly cut themselves adrift spiritually.

Over the years, I have watched these people try to navigate life with no moral compass, no reliable scale to weigh right from wrong, no sound guidance on how to raise their kids, love their spouse, thrive at work, or find God. Time and again, I have seen these bright, promising people shipwreck their lives through painful divorces, addictive behaviors, dysfunctional relationships, and financial mismanagement—all because they were trying to live their lives apart from the Author of life.

When I see people dash their lives against the rocks because no one has ever cared enough to come alongside them and show them a better way, it breaks my heart. I know it doesn't have to be that way. There is a God whose love is so high, so deep, so wide, and so pure, it transforms human hearts and changes human destinies.

That's my why. God has placed it in my heart to go to people like this, my friends who are far from God and may not even know it. God has given me a special responsibility for people like this. Their spiritual state weighs on me. Back in the day, it was called a "burden." No matter what I do, I can't break free from it. The truth is, I don't want to.

Has the mission of Jesus seeped into your heart? When the love of Christ touches you by faith and you allow his love to get a hold of you, it will change your why. You will see in a new light how much people matter to God. You won't be able to stand it that people are drifting far from God and shuffling through this world unloved. That scenario will become unacceptable to you. Love will compel you to do something about it, perhaps something no one has ever done before. You'll decide to "be more vile" and go where the people are, not just geographically, but in other ways, too. You will meet them on their turf and their terms, and you will intentionally share the good news of Jesus in ways they can understand, which we'll talk about next. As a bonus, you'll feel fully alive because for the first time, you'll be living your why.

Prayer
Lord, give me a heart that breaks with compassion when I encounter people who don't know you and a desire to meet them where they are.

Hiding God's Word in My Heart
The size of the harvest is bigger than you can imagine, but there are few workers. Therefore, plead with the Lord of the harvest to send out workers for his harvest.

—Jesus, Matthew 9:37-38 (CEB)

Discussion guide available at www.MeetTheGoodpeople.com.

Chapter Three

Plain Talk

A word fitly spoken is like apples of gold in a setting of silver.

—Proverbs 25:11

Think like a wise man but communicate in the language of the people.

—William Butler Yeats

Have you ever tried to talk to someone who doesn't speak your language? Several years ago, I was on a crowded train in southern Spain. The man standing six inches from me had something pressing to say.

"*Sprechen Sie Deutsch?*" he asked.

I said, "No. English?"

"No," he responded. "*Parlez-vous français?*"

"No," I replied. I speak a little bit of Spanish, so I took one more shot. "*¿Hablas español?*"

"No," he answered. "*Italiano?*"

"No."

In a matter of seconds, we riffled through five languages, searching for a common channel to communicate, but it wasn't on the dial. Finally, with great frustration in his eyes, he shrugged his shoulders and gave up. For the rest of the ride, we stood next to each other in silence. I still wonder what he so urgently wanted to tell me. (I was probably standing on his foot.)

Maybe you know what it's like to have something vitally important to say, but the other person simply doesn't speak your language.

28

If you are a Christian in America, you know this experience all too well. The moment you introduce the topic of faith, you will likely be standing next to someone who has no vocabulary for the conversation. Ironically, while the culture's interest in spirituality is peaking, basic knowledge of Christianity is on the decline.

This seeming contradiction may explain the surprising popularity of the Bible on box office and home TV screens in recent times. Hollywood's versions of *Noah, The Bible,* and *Son of God* have led millions of people to watch the Word. Such shows uncover a hidden desire to know what the Bible says about God and how to relate to God without plodding through dusty pages filled with words and history that most people don't understand.

In their 2014 "State of the Bible" study, the Barna Group and the American Bible Society found some revealing trends about the Good Book.[1] In just three years, the percentage of Americans who view the Bible as sacred literature has dropped seven points from 86 percent in 2011 to 79 percent in 2014. At the same time, there has been a dramatic rise in what the study calls "Bible skeptics." The number of people who believe the Bible is "just another book of teachings written by men that contains stories and advice" has nearly doubled from 10 percent to 19 percent. For the first time since tracking began in 2011, Bible skeptics now equal the number of people considered "Bible engaged"—those who read the Bible at least four times a week and believe it is the actual or inspired word of God. The emerging millennial generation, defined as ages eighteen to twenty-nine, is leading this shift toward skepticism. While 50 percent of all adults believe the Bible has too little influence in society, only 30 percent of millennials believe this.[2]

A related trend is "The Rise of the Nones." Decades ago a research team at the University of Chicago began tracking Americans' religious affiliation. They asked, "What is your religious preference?" and gave the following choices: Protestant, Catholic, Jewish, some other religion, or no religion. In 1972, 5 percent of Americans said, "no religion." By 1990, that number crept up to 8 percent.[3] But by 2014, the number of Americans reporting "no religion" had nearly tripled to 22.8 percent.[4] Something happened in the quarter-century following 1990. Previously, people who did not attend a specific church reported the church they attended as a child or their family's connection to the Baptist or Catholic Church, regardless of how distant the tie. That's no longer the case.

News of the "nones" has touched off a great debate. Many social commentators have declared that Americans are disavowing religion in unprecedented numbers. Others say people may simply be answering more honestly. University of Chicago researchers were careful to distinguish between those who claimed "no religion," meaning no connection to an organized religion, and those who considered themselves atheist. Only 3 percent of those interviewed were atheists and just 8 percent said they were raised with no religion.[5] Whether people are disavowing religion or being more honest about it, one thing is clear: there's a rising sense of disconnection from organized religion. The culture is changing—quickly.

In this whirlwind, Christianity is getting lost in translation. Increasingly, postmodern people don't speak the language. They don't know the stories, themes, or key figures in the Bible, and they are blissfully unaware of Christian history or tradition. George Hunter calls them "ignostics": they simply don't know what Christians are talking about.[6] To most Americans, redemption is what you do with food stamps, King James came back to play for Cleveland, and Grace is a blue-eyed blonde.

This translation problem is showing up in other parts of the world, too. Ever watched Monty Python? (It's OK. You can admit it.) According to a senior figure at the BBC, the British public has such "poor religious literacy" that a modern audience would be stumped by the Monty Python film *The Life of Brian*—a comic parody on the life of Jesus. They wouldn't understand the biblical references.

Aaqil Ahmed, the BBC's head of religion and ethics, claims that meager religious education over two generations has left people without a basic knowledge of Christianity or other religions. In an interview, he wondered if people today would get that "great joke about the Sermon on the Mount" in the 1979 Python flick where a woman asks, "What's so special about the cheesemakers?" It was referring to Jesus's words, "Blessed are the peacemakers."[7] (It's a lot funnier in the movie.)

With the culture rapidly changing and basic knowledge of the Christian faith disappearing, we have entered a new era in the West. Christians are now missionaries in their own backyard. Those of us who follow Christ must assume that people in our office, school, worksite, neighborhood, and even our home have no vocabulary of faith. If we want to communicate with them, the good news must be reborn in the language of twenty-first-century culture.

A friend of mine serves as an international missionary for Wycliffe Bible Translators. Although she grew up in Illinois and has lived in the United States her whole life, she's been assigned to Tanzania in East Africa. Her team lives among the Burunge tribe to learn their language and culture. Their goal is to translate the Bible into words the people can understand. The Burunge people are one of approximately 1,860 people groups in the world who do not have a Bible translation in their native language.[8] Increasingly, postmodern people in America fall into that same category. By some estimates, it's a tribe 180 million strong.

How can we translate the Christian faith into a language our nonchurched friends, neighbors, and coworkers understand? It starts by leading with our deeds.

Lead with Deeds

Talk is cheap. We've all known persons who talk a good game but don't back it up with their actions. There's something inauthentic about that. Most of us want to get past the hype and find out if the "product" being promoted really makes a difference in a person's life. Words alone are rarely able to do this. When it comes to faith, it's better to show the good news before you say it.

One cold February morning, a group from our church stood in front of the county courthouse in Springfield to show God's love in a practical way. As people sloshed through the snow, we gave away cups of hot chocolate and homemade cookies to anyone who passed by.

For many people, it was a huge hit. Their day or maybe their life had run low on kindness. To receive some hot cocoa and a cookie without having to earn it or deserve it brought a sudden smile to their face and a spring to their step. For others, it was too good to be true. "What are you doing this for?" they asked over and over. It was an easy answer. "For you. To show you God's love."

Of course, there were some who put their heads down and walked past with barely a "No, thank you." That was OK. We made the offer. We had some other reactions as well. One guy saw our sign: "FREE HOT COCOA!" and said, "What's she in for?"

Later that day someone sent this message through our website: "What a nice surprise to have a cup of hot cocoa handed to me as

I walked in to work at the County Building this morning! It tasted really good when I warmed it up at 10:30! Sorry that there were those who were really skeptical of your mission. We get approached by some mighty strange people around our building. Thanks again. You made me smile!"

No offense was taken. Knee-jerk skepticism is normal when complete strangers offer you hot cocoa for no apparent reason. Here's what jumps to mind: "Why would someone do this? What are they after?" That's precisely what makes a demonstration of God's grace so disarming. It's not done to get something. It's done to give something. Most people are wired for transaction. "I'll give you this, if you give me that." To receive an act of kindness with no strings attached softens the heart.

Somehow nonchurched people implicitly know that real faith is both good news and good deeds. It includes both truth and proof. But to unlock the door of a skeptic's heart, we must lead with deeds. Deep down, spiritually curious people are saying, "Don't give me words. Let me see your faith. I want to know the difference it makes in your life. When I see you do something for others out of love and not self-interest, then I'll listen to what you say."

A couple of months after our kindness outreach, a woman shook my hand after one of our worship services and said, "I received one of those cups of hot chocolate back in February. I think you gave it to me. Later, I realized this church is not far from my home. I've been going through some changes in my life, and I thought I would try it out. I liked it. I'll be back."

We win people's hearts with humble deeds. When writing to the early Christians in Rome, Paul says it is God's kindness that leads us to a change of heart and life.[9]

Demonstrations of God's kindness gave incredible dynamism to the early Methodist movement. In the early 1740s, John Wesley and his fledgling followers bought an abandoned cannon foundry in London and renovated it to become Methodism's home base in Great Britain. The new Methodist society at the Foundry included powerful expressions of kindness and mercy. Wesley established what we would call a microlending fund. He made small loans to 250 people in that first year. The poor received basic medical care each Friday. Poor and elderly widows and their children found a place to stay in two houses leased by the Foundry. A school was started for street children.[10] For Wesley, it was simply faith working through love.[11] He connected an inward experience of Christ's love with an outward expression of Christlike kindness. Truth and proof. It's a powerful combination.

Then as now, faith in action earns us the right to be heard. When that door cracks open, it's a sacred moment. To make the most of it, we must speak in a language they know.

Keep It Simple

Which makes you sound more intelligent, using long words or short ones? Most people would say long. That's what researcher Daniel Oppenheimer found when he polled Stanford undergraduates. When asked if they had ever changed words in an academic essay so it would sound more intelligent, 86 percent said yes. They're not alone. But the more interesting question is, "Does it work?" Do longer words make a person sound more intelligent?

We now have proof that they don't. You get a hint of this in Oppenheimer's tongue-in-cheek title: "Consequences of Erudite Vernacular Utilized Irrespective of Necessity: Problems with Using Long Words Needlessly." The study asked seventy-one Stanford students to evaluate "highly complex" writing samples and simpler texts with the same content. Surprisingly, complexity led people to consider the author less intelligent. Oppenheimer's conclusion: "Write clearly and simply if you can, and you'll be more likely to be thought of as intelligent."[12]

Many Christians suffer from a complexity complex. They feel a need to sound intelligent as they talk about their faith. To make matters worse, there are a lot of long words in Christianity: *prevenient, justification, sanctification, glorification,* and so on. It is easy to throw around vocabulary that people outside the faith don't understand. Yet when Jesus spoke, the common people heard him gladly.[13] He knew how to speak their language.

Not everyone does. It certainly didn't come naturally to young John. Wesley grew up a pastor's kid. Both his father Samuel and mother Susanna were bright, well-educated, and insatiable learners. From a tender age, John absorbed the vocabulary of faith. He later became an Oxford scholar deeply steeped in the Christian tradition and a priest in the Church of England. Yet his burning passion over six decades of ministry was to communicate the gospel to the masses—most of whom were illiterate. To do so, he left behind the language of the academy. "I design plain truth for plain people," he said. "I labour to avoid all words which are not easy to be understood, all which are not used in common life."[14]

Although Wesley's ability to connect with everyday people became legendary, he didn't start that way. As a young preacher, he gave a sophisticated sermon to a country congregation that fell flat. He knew by the looks on their faces they had not understood him. Undeterred, he crossed out some of the long words and gave it another shot. This time they looked only half as confused.

Wesley wanted better. He read his sermon to a maidservant and asked her to interrupt him each time she didn't understand. Wesley was shocked by the number of times Betsy said, "Stop, sir." All his education had created a barrier to sharing Christ with everyday people. He resolved at that point to replace long words with short ones until people could understand his every word.[15]

Wesley counseled his preachers to do the same. Listen to the conversation he had with Rev. Samuel Furley.

> Clearness in particular is necessary for you and me, because we are to instruct people of the lowest understanding. Therefore we, above all, if we think with the wise, yet must speak with the vulgar [meaning "ordinary"]. We should constantly use the most common, little, easy words (so they are pure and proper) which our language affords. When I had been a member of the university about ten years, I wrote and talked much as you do now. But when I talked to plain people in the Castle or the town, I observed they gaped and stared. This quickly obliged me to alter my style and adopt the language of those I spoke to. And yet there is a dignity in this simplicity, which is not disagreeable to those of the highest rank.[16]

It's the easiest thing in the world to assume that a word familiar to us is familiar to everyone else. But gone are the days when we can assume people in American culture understand Christian code words like *sin, grace, salvation, repentance,* or *holiness.* When we use them without defining them in simple terms, we are speaking a language nonchurched people don't understand.

How do you learn the language of the people? Watch some TV. Listen to the number one radio station in your area. Go to the movie everyone's talking about. Read some magazines at the grocery store checkout. Talk to a teenager. My seventeen-year-old daughter is more than happy to tell me when I am using words she doesn't understand or phrases that have passed their expiration date. ("Dad, really?!") If you don't have a teenager in your house, rent one. Take two or three of them out to eat and let them tell you what life looks like through their eyes. As you listen, you may discover the best way to speak their language.

Invite Them into a Conversation

Once you learn the words that connect, use them in conversations. Get to know some of the Goodpeople in your life a little better. An easy way is to invite them out to eat. In a former church, we invited people to sign up for something we called "Dinner for 8." We put together four couples or eight single persons and said, "Go have dinner together at least four times." They could go out to eat or have dinner at someone's home—their choice. We gave them no material or agenda other than to get to know one another.

My wife, Leanne, and I were thrown in a group with some women who came to church each week without their husbands. Somehow these women got their husbands to agree to come to these dinners—which shows just how persuasive wives can be.

Given the circumstances, no one knew how the first dinner would go. To everyone's surprise, it was an absolute grand slam. We talked and laughed and swapped stories until way past our ending time, and that started something. The group kept meeting every two or three months, just for dinner. Over time, one of the couples had to drop out for family reasons, but the rest of us went on for a couple of years.

As I got to know the other two men, I discovered they were great guys. One was really funny, and the other was a great listener. They were good husbands, hard workers, and adamantly opposed to church. As a result, we didn't talk about church or faith or God during our dinners, unless they brought it up—which was rare.

In fact, when we stopped having our dinners, those guys still didn't want much to do with church. But we had become friends. Sometime after that, both of them accepted Christ. Now they are each involved in a small group, personally studying to grow in their faith each day, and actively serving in that church and community. One of them wants to lead a thirty-four-week intensive study of the

Bible in the homeless shelter in his city. Their transformation has been astounding.

Without a doubt, God used their wives to do the spiritual heavy lifting. Their quiet witness and faithful prayers carried the day. But God also sparked something during those two years of dinner parties. Some of the hardness in their hearts melted just enough to receive the love they always wanted but somehow thought was beyond their reach.

Too often we focus on presenting our faith. We work hard at stating the good news in the clearest way possible and hope people will respond the moment they hear it. In reality, the core message of the Christian faith needs to be explained, modeled, tested, and questioned in a safe, back-and-forth dialogue. It takes time for the pieces to come together. Like cooking a gourmet meal, it can't be rushed. To share it, you have to get up close and stay there awhile. Christianity has always been more caught than taught. That's why relational faith sharing can mark a person so profoundly. People want to be invited into a conversation.

Among all the other things he did, Wesley was well-known as a conversationalist. Alexander Pope wrote, "I hate to meet up with John Wesley. The dog enchants you with his conversation, and breaks it off to go talk to an old woman."[17]

Wesley considered personal conversations a major part of his ministry. They were often conducted through letters. Perhaps this explains why more than 2,600 of Wesley's letters have been collected to date. Time and again, he found that something of the Spirit was translated on a deeper level in personal exchanges. In his journal he wrote, "After all our preaching, many of our people are almost as ignorant as if they had never heard the gospel. . . . I have found by experience, that one of these has learned more from one hour's close discourse than from ten years' public preaching."[18]

My experience has mirrored Wesley's countless times. Most recently it was with a man I'll call Bill. A gentle man in his late seventies, Bill was recently diagnosed with a terminal illness. His stated reason to talk with me involved an issue in his family. Once we covered that topic and talked through his health situation, I asked him about his son. I said, "Bill, I'd like to help your son have a more conscious contact with God."

Immediately he said, "That's what I want!"

It caught me off guard. Bill has been a faithful member of the church his whole life. I asked him if he had ever invited Christ into his life.

He said, "No. I just kind of went along through life. I always tried to do the right thing and be a good person, but I never had a personal relationship with God. I've tried to love God and show God my love. I think God loves me. I've just never had that relationship."

"Would you like to have it?" I asked.

He said, "Yes!"

For the next few moments, this precious man who has listened to sermons for over seventy years and tried his whole life to do the right thing bowed his head. In his own words, he invited Jesus to do for him what he could not do for himself. As he finished praying, he finally felt loved. The joy on Bill's face and the confidence he has in his savior seem stronger each time I see him. He inspires me.

We can translate the Christian faith into a language our non-churched friends and family can understand. Our deeds of kindness can soften their hearts toward spiritual things. If we will then invite them into a conversation and use words that make sense to them, Jesus will do the rest.

Prayer

Lord, teach me how to listen and talk to people in a way they can understand, and give me opportunities to enter into conversations that change lives.

Hiding God's Word in My Heart
The large crowd listened to [Jesus] with delight.

—Mark 12:37b (CEB)

Discussion guide available at www.MeetTheGoodpeople.com.

+& Chapter Four &+

Tune In to Their Hearts

When I walked in to the sanctuary a feeling came over me
like I've never had before. I was home. When the music started
I had goose bumps, and I had them the entire service. I've never felt that
way in church.

—Sheri, 32

Sooner or later, it was bound to happen. Remember our friends Joe and Sally Goodpeople? Life threw them a curve. Their youngest son was in a freak accident that threatened his life. Fortunately, he was able to recover, but the experience shook their family to the core. One day as they were driving to a soccer game, Sally said softly, "I think we should go to church this Sunday." Joe wasn't too excited about the idea, but he knew how much the accident had scared them both, and it brought up a lot of questions they couldn't answer.

The next Sunday they showed up at a church not far from their house. Once inside, a gentleman in a suit and tie handed them a folded piece of paper with a bunch of stuff inside and gently smiled as they walked in the sanctuary. The room was about half full with an older crowd. The organ was playing softly. The lights were dim. Even Joe had to admit it was calming.

As the service started, there were several announcements about meetings and activities for the members. The songs were not familiar, of course, because this family had never sung hymns. At one point, a lively choir sang a beautiful piece from the late 1800s. The pastor's sermon was informative and well presented, but Joe and Sally weren't sure what they were supposed to do with it. After the service, a couple of people nodded and smiled at them while most were caught up in conversations with those they already knew. The entire morning was very nice. It just felt like it was for someone else. They never went back.

A month later, one of Joe's friends at work mentioned playing in the band at his church. It caught Joe off guard. "What do you mean you play in the band?" His friend explained that his church used a lot of rock and pop-style music, and he played bass guitar a couple of Sundays a month. This piqued Joe's interest. Flipping through scenes in his mind, he said slowly, "You know, I played drums in a band for years until our first child was born." His friend said, "Why don't you come and check it out?"

A couple of Sundays later, he did. After a twenty-five-minute drive, the family pulled into the church parking and were immediately greeted by smiling parking attendants in orange vests. When they came to the main entrance, other people were there to open the doors and warmly welcome them. Once inside, a young woman in casual clothes gave them a half-sheet of paper and a cheery, "Welcome to worship today," as they entered the worship center.

By this time, the band was gearing up and people were standing, moving with the music. As a younger crowd filed in, they could feel the energy. The songs were not familiar, of course, because this family had never sung contemporary Christian songs. But they recognized the beat. The music made them feel at home, and the words were easy to follow on the large screens in front. At one point, a video clip showed a local mission opportunity open to anyone wanting to make a difference. The pastor's sermon was conversational with some humor sprinkled in. Halfway through a woman told a powerful story about her struggles and how God moved in her life to change things. At the end, the pastor gave some clear next steps.

After the service, a couple noticed Joe and Sally, introduced themselves, and offered to answer any questions about the church. The couple then thanked them for coming and offered their e-mail addresses if Joe or Sally ever wanted to talk further. The whole experience was far beyond what they expected. When they got in their car, Joe turned to Sally and said, "I know this isn't true, but it felt like the entire service was made for us."

To connect with significant numbers of nonchurched people, we must tune in to the heart of their culture. In particular, we must tune in to their music. This is the next step in Wesley's model for sharing faith. Let's recap the journey so far.

First: Pray for a change in our hearts and the hearts of those far from God.

Second: Go where the people are. Meet them on their turf and their terms.

Third: Learn to speak their language and engage them in conversations about a life-changing relationship with Jesus.

The fourth step is to provide forms of worship that tune in to their hearts. To seriously commit to this next step, we must answer this question: Do nonchurched people have to become like us before they can become Christian? In other words, must they adopt our culture to adopt our faith? This was the debate that nearly tripped the church right out of the gate.

The early church was initially composed of Jewish persons who became Christians, worshipping Jesus as their Messiah. As this new community of believers took shape in Jerusalem, there was such awestruck power, unity, and generosity that new people were turning their lives over to Christ every day.[1] From time to time, some Gentiles became Christians, too. Because they were a small minority, they simply adapted to the customs and culture of Jewish Christians. They kept the Jewish law, ate kosher foods, and the men were circumcised as a sign of God's covenant with the Jewish people.[2]

When persecution scattered the believers in Jerusalem to the surrounding areas of Judea and beyond, many more Gentiles heard the good news and became followers of Christ. Missionary work further changed the landscape. To their great surprise, both Peter and Paul witnessed God give the gift of the Holy Spirit to the Gentiles just as to the Jews.[3] Amazingly, God showed no partiality, and the faith quickly spread beyond the confines of Judaism.

News of Gentile populations becoming Christ followers without submitting to Jewish laws and customs infuriated some of the Jewish Christians in Judea. After all, Jesus was a Jew. He was the fulfillment of Jewish law and prophecy. He was the Jewish Messiah. These

"Judaizers" drew a hard line in the sand: to become Christians, all Gentiles must become Jews first.[4] To them, it only made sense.

With tensions rising, James, the leader of the Jerusalem church, called a meeting of the minds. As they gathered in Jerusalem, Peter shared how God had worked and urged the assembly not to place a burden on the Gentiles that even the Jews could not bear. Salvation did not come through following the law but through receiving God's unmerited love offered in Jesus Christ.[5] Paul argued strongly against imposing one culture on every people group. Jesus had come to save the world, not a single nation.

In the end, the leaders sided with Peter and Paul. The Christian faith was for everyone in every culture. That single decision changed the trajectory of Christianity from an obscure sect of Judaism to a global movement of God.

Through this process, the early church made a brilliant discovery: *people connect most easily with the gospel when it comes through their native culture.* We know this now as the "indigenous principle," and each time the church has practiced it, the faith has spread to people and groups who had never been reached.

One might think the Jerusalem Council settled this matter once and for all. No one should have to adopt someone else's culture to adopt the faith. But it seems the Judaizers are with us in every generation. It's in our nature. We're prone to hang on to the familiar, what has worked in the past, what God used to reach us, and we think it should work for everyone. But it doesn't. Culture changes. New generations are born. Social contracts are rewritten. Although the word of God doesn't change, the world around us is changing at warp speed. To tune into the hearts of nonchurched people, we must constantly be adapting to a new reality. This is especially true with our worship forms.

The Real Christians

When life feels like a blur, we instinctively entrench. For Christians, our first line of defense is often our style of worship. We drive a stake in the ground and say, "This is what it means to be a real Christian. You must adopt our style to adopt our faith." Of course, we don't do this maliciously or even intentionally. We simply get comfortable with a certain form of worship over time, and it becomes "normal" to us. Once our definition of normal sets in, it's easy to confuse personal taste with universal truth. This is especially true when it comes to musical taste.

An old farmer went to the city one weekend and attended a large church. He came home and his wife asked him how it was.

"Well," said the farmer, "it was good. They did something different, however. They sang praise choruses instead of hymns."

"Praise choruses?" said his wife. "What are those?"

"Oh, they're okay. They're sort of like hymns, only different," said the farmer.

"Well, what's the difference?" asked his wife.

The farmer said, "Well, it's like this—If I were to say to you: 'Martha, the cows are in the corn,' well that would be a hymn.

"If, on the other hand, I were to say to you: 'Martha Martha, Martha, Oh, Martha, MARTHA, MARTHA, the cows, the big cows, the brown cows, the black cows, the white cows, the black and white cows, the COWS, COWS, COWS are in the corn, are in the corn, are in the corn, are in the corn, the CORN, CORN, CORN.'

"Then, if I were to repeat the whole thing two or three times, well that would be a praise chorus."

Coincidentally, the same week, a young businessman from the city who normally attended a church with contemporary-style worship, was in the old farmer's town on business and visited the farmer's small town church.

He came home and his wife asked him how it was. "Well," said the young man, "it was good. They did something different, however. They sang hymns instead of regular songs."

"Hymns?" said his wife. "What are those?"

"Oh, they're okay. They're sort of like regular songs, only different," said the young man.

"Well, what's the difference?" asked his wife.

The young man said, "Well, it's like this—If I were to say to you, 'Martha, the cows are in the corn,' that would be a regular song. If, on the other hand, I were to say to you:

Oh Martha, dear Martha, hear thou my cry
Inclinest thine ear to the words of my mouth.
Turn thou thy whole wondrous ear by and by
to the righteous, inimitable, glorious truth.

For the way of the animals who can explain,
There in their heads is no shadow of sense.
Hearkenest they in God's sun or his rain
Unless from the mild, tempting corn they are fenced.

Yea those cows in glad bovine, rebellious delight,
Have broke free their shackles, their warm pens eschewed.
Then goaded by minions of darkness and night,
They all my mild Chilliwack sweet corn have chewed.

So look to that bright shining day by and by,
Where all foul corruptions of earth are reborn.
Where no vicious animal makes my soul cry.
And I no longer see those foul cows in the corn.

Then, if I were to do only verses one, three and four and do a key change on the last verse, well that would be a hymn."[6]

Notice that both men thought their worship form was "normal." In each case, the core message was the same: "Martha, the cows are in the corn." But they each felt the "other" expression of that message was foreign to who they were. Was either expression wrong? Of course not. They were simply tailored to different cultures. The question is not "Who are the real Christians?" but rather, "Who are we trying to reach?"

Indigenous Faith

Every worship experience is designed to reach a certain group of people. Unfortunately, in most cases the design unintentionally excludes nonchurched people. It either repeats what was created long ago for a different culture, or it reflects the preferred worship style of the people who currently attend a particular church. In both cases, the focus is on what is best for the people who are already there, rather than those who aren't there yet. It also assumes the experience is attractive to nonchurched people today. Ed Stetzer and Mike Dodson claim, "All churches are culturally relevant; the question is whether they are relevant to a culture that currently exists in their community or to one that disappeared generations ago."[7]

Every time a nonchurched person adopts a style of worship designed for long-term insiders, it's a throwback to first-century Gentiles becoming Jews to become Christians. It will succeed occasionally, but the vast majority of the culture will be lost. How does a group or a church begin to think intentionally about designing a worship experience for postmodern people who don't go to church? Tune in to their hearts.

My friend Lauren was skittish about faith. Every time the subject came up, she preferred to talk about other things. One day I suggested listening to the local Christian music station when she wasn't doing anything else. She didn't have to believe everything they were singing, but at least the messages would be positive in this often negative world. With nothing to lose, she gave it a try. As she was driving or doing things around the house, she played the station in the background. She was quick to say she didn't catch all the lyrics, but she enjoyed the music. Over time, her heart softened. She became more open to spiritual conversations. About a year later, Lauren became a Christian.

Music is one of the easiest ways to tune in to a person's heart. It often slips past the frontal lobe of rational control and touches an inner place of tenderness and need. It can calm, excite, inspire, and embolden. As it washes over us, music can lower our resistance and make us more receptive to a life-changing message. My friend Lauren isn't the only one who's had issues with faith. Tens of millions are just like her. Could we harness this powerful force in our worship experiences to lead pre-Christian people to faith in Christ?

Whether we are into church or not, when someone plays "our music," something inside us springs to life. My eighty-eight-year-old neighbor is deeply devoted to his Lutheran church. As a lifelong member, he dearly loves singing the great hymns of the faith. But when he gets in his car, this dear churchman will be tapping his toes to a CD of the Glen Miller Band. That's his heart language. Had he never set foot in a church, the best way to connect with his soul would have been through the snappy tunes of big band music, not "A Mighty Fortress Is Our God."

What's the music that connects with your soul? It's often related to what was popular when you came of age or what you were exposed to on a regular basis. If you spent a lot of time in a traditional worship setting and associate it with warm memories of family and friends, chances are high you will connect with God through traditional church music. It soothes your soul, even if it's not the music you would choose to listen to in your car. Naturally, pre-Christian people with no church background have not acquired that taste. When John Wesley stumbled upon this reality nearly three centuries ago, it changed his entire approach to music.

Although eighteenth-century England was a churchy culture, the church had long since lost the English masses. To them, church was divorced from real life. The dress, language, customs, and music were all designed for the upper crust of society, not "commoners."

As a priest in the Church of England, John Wesley had become part of that establishment. He was quite fond of the high church liturgy, the ancient hymns, and the formal prayers. But his heart-warming experience at Aldersgate and his insistence on salvation by faith led most clergy to ban him from their pulpits. Undaunted, he went straight to the people. He spoke outdoors to the masses in Kingswood and other places and soon realized the need for songs that would connect with his mostly "uncultured" listeners. That's when he turned to his brother Charles, a budding poet.

Although Charles was not a musician and never wrote a note of music, he intentionally set his poems to the popular tunes of the day.[8] In most cases, they were songs written by contemporary composers and no doubt lustily sung in the English pubs. When Charles put gospel words to "Top 40" tunes, it caught the hearts of nonchurched people like never before. For the first time, they didn't have to become someone else to become Christian. It was church for them. Charles tuned in to their heart language, and it helped these left-out people finally feel at home.

Our time is also filled with people who feel like church is for someone else. In their book *Churchless*, George Barna and David Kinnaman share recent research based on interviews with more than 20,500 adults across America, including over 6,000 adults who do not attend church. The data revealed a troubling trend: "The younger the generation, the more post-Christian it is."[9] Each new wave of American society is less connected to Christian identity, belief, and practice than the one before. That shouldn't be a shock to most people. The surprising part is how rapidly the tide is rising.

- Elders (born in 1945 or earlier)—28 percent post-Christian

- Boomers (born between 1946 and 1964)—35 percent post-Christian

- Busters (born between 1965 and 1983)—40 percent post-Christian

- Mosaics (born between 1984 and 2002)—48 percent post-Christian[10]

What is the best way to connect these precious people with the forgiveness and love of Jesus Christ? Follow the approach of the Wesleys: pray for them, meet them on their turf and terms, learn to speak their language, and create indigenous forms of worship that tune in to their hearts.

Jesus told his followers, "Go and make disciples of all nations."[11] Nations are simply "people groups": rich, poor, young, old, Hispanic, Asian, chocolate lovers, and chocolate loathers (this is a small people group). These days many Christ followers are finding "nations" that have been left out of church.

In rural areas of the American Midwest and ranching regions in the West and Southwest, churches are springing up with a distinctive mission: to reach people connected to country living. "Cowboy Church" invites people in blue jeans, boots, and cowboy hats to worship God in their heart language—country and western.

A church in the inner city of Minneapolis uses hip-hop to reach young people looking for hope that overcomes drugs and gangs.

Hillsong Church in Australia has spawned chart-topping praise and worship songs for many years, drawing new generations to Christ. Now the Sydney megachurch is planting churches in major cities around the world. They're using "rock concert" worship experiences to connect with urban young adults by the tens of thousands. Hillsong has locations in Barcelona, Berlin, Cape Town, Kiev, New York, London, Los Angeles, Paris, Stockholm, and other global hotspots.[12]

North Coast Church in North San Diego County takes this indigenous principle to a completely different level. In the 1990s, as one of the earliest multisite churches in America, they began offering multiple worship services in different venues. Although many churches now have multiple sites for worship, North Coast's variety makes them unique. Each weekend in Vista, California, they offer nineteen worship services in nine different worship styles.

When you visit their website, northcoastchurch.com, you are encouraged to "pick the worship service and style that works for you." It's like a multiplex theater showing a variety of movies at assorted times. North Coast's worship music styles "vary from traditional hymns and choruses to contemporary songs, from Country Gospel bluegrass to THE EDGE, a cutting-edge experience incorporating electric guitars and high energy worship." There's also a "Soul Gospel" service described as "groove oriented, gospel centered music with a touch of soul" and a service with extended reflective music after the message.[13] Each service hears the same sermon by the pastor, either in person or by video teaching, and each style connects with a different group of people.

It's the same lesson the Wesleys learned. Churches that lead large numbers of pre-Christian people to Christ employ the music of the group they are trying to reach. They know people connect most easily with the gospel when it comes through their native culture. It's their heart language. One formerly nonchurched person in my community described her experience this way:

> Sunday worship for me is utter release. I am so caught up in the "world" all week, and I usually can't wait for church. Just walking into the building is exhilarating and I really look forward to the message. Honestly though, what gets me more than anything is the music. I have always had a soulful connection with music, and now the relationship I have with the Lord has magnified the feelings I get from it.
>
> There are times I am so moved by the Holy Spirit while singing, I can't even sing anymore. I am so overwhelmed with the words and feelings of gratitude all I can do is cry. I have a hard time putting these thoughts on paper, because I have NEVER felt like this before. I want nothing more than to thank First Church for being so welcoming and loving. I wouldn't trade this in for all the money in the world!

Maybe the Wesleys were on to something. What group is God calling you to reach: single moms, retirees, addicts, young professionals, migrant workers? Find out what they listen to and include that music in your worship experiences. If we want pre-Christian people to hear our words, we'll have to tune in to their hearts.

Prayer
Lord Jesus, give me eyes to see those times when I have told people they have to become like me before they can become your follower.

Hiding God's Word in My Heart
We believe that we and they are saved in the same way, by the grace of the Lord Jesus.

—Acts 15:11 (CEB)

Discussion guide available at www.MeetTheGoodpeople.com.

✥ Chapter Five ✣

Do Life Together

The Bible knows nothing of solitary religion.

—John Wesley

"Please God, all I want is one. I just want one person to hang out with. It doesn't have to be magical, and we don't have to be best friends or anything. I just want a friend. Please, open my eyes to who this one person might be. Show me someone who would be a good friend for me!"

That was Taisia's prayer on her way to church one morning. The intensity of her desire surprised even her. About five years before, she had moved from Minnesota to Illinois to marry the love of her life, a man she first met online. They bought a home, made a life, and were deliriously happy. But something was missing. Over several months, Taisia began to feel depressed. It made no sense to her. "This was supposed to be my happily ever after and everything I prayed for!" she said. "What right did I have to feel this way? Why on earth was I so empty and sad?"

Sensing a need, she and her husband started attending our church. One Sunday Taisia heard a message about the power of a small group and having friends to do life with. "It hit me like a ton of bricks," she said. "I felt myself shrink in the pew and struggled to hold back my tears. That's exactly what was going on! I had all these amazing things happening and no one in my corner locally to share in my joys and my challenges. I was experiencing something I wasn't all that familiar with, loneliness."

She's not alone. Loneliness is on the rise in America. In a recent survey, 40 percent of adults age forty-five and over said they were

48

lonely. That's double the percentage who reported loneliness in the 1980s.[1] Ironically, this dramatic increase in inner isolation has been simultaneous with an explosion in social media. Facebook, for instance, connects over 500 million daily users around the world in social interaction. Yet a recent study found that the greater the amount of time spent on Facebook, the less happy you feel throughout the day.[2] How could that be?

Sherry Turkle, a professor at MIT and author of *Alone Together: Why We Expect More from Technology and Less from Each Other*, has spent over fifteen years studying how our "plugged-in lives" have changed who we are. She claims that all of our technological devices have produced a world in which we're always communicating, but we're seldom having real conversations.

According to Turkle, we're a nation of sippers. "We are tempted to think that our little 'sips' of online connection add up to a big gulp of real conversation," she says. "But they don't. E-mail, Twitter, Facebook, all of these have their places. . . . But no matter how valuable, they do not substitute for conversation. Connecting in sips may work for gathering discrete bits of information or for saying, 'I am thinking about you.' . . . But connecting in sips doesn't work as well when it comes to understanding and knowing one another."[3]

Intuitively, we know this. I may not have had the privilege of meeting you yet. We may have never texted each other or connected on Facebook, but I know your greatest need. It is the same as mine. Our greatest human need is to be understood—to be known and accepted by someone for who we are. It's the restless longing that drives our constant flow of electronic sips. We are afraid of being alone.

It's in Our DNA

Of course, this isn't new. Our quest for connection runs deep because we were created for community from the beginning. As God was creating human beings in the second chapter of Genesis, the Lord quickly recognized something about the first man. No matter how many creatures God brought before Adam, none of them filled the emptiness inside. Adam could name them, but he couldn't love them.

Until this point, everything God had created was good. There was light; it was good. There was dry land; it was good. The sun and the moon, plants and animals—good, good, all good! But when the Lord saw that the man was alone, for the first time God said, "Not good."

"Then the LORD God said, 'It is not good that the man should be alone. I will make him a helper as his partner.'"[4]

Keep in mind that this sense of aloneness is before sin enters the world. Adam is in a beautiful garden with all of his needs cared for and is living in perfect harmony with God and the rest of creation. Yet something is missing. Without human companionship, the man could not experience the fullness of humanity. In fact, when companionship is withheld, it literally changes the way our bodies work. I learned this from a little guy named Alek.

In April one year, a young couple in the church I was serving adopted a beautiful, two-year-old boy from Ukraine. Until that time, Alek had lived in a state-run children's home with three hundred kids all under the age of five.

In August, his mom took him for one of his regular physical checkups. When the doctor came in to look over Alek's chart, it showed he had grown five inches in four months. The doctor said, "That can't be."

They measured Alek again, and it was true. He had grown five inches in the four months he had lived with his new parents, who had showered him with love and attention (not to mention a little food). The doctor told his mom, "I have heard of children 'thriving' when put in a loving environment, but I have never seen it—until now."

Community is in our DNA. It's sown into our cells. "Harvard researcher Robert Putnam notes that if you belong to no groups but decide to join one, 'you can cut your risk of dying over the next year *in half*.'"[5] Imagine going to an insurance agent and saying, "I would like a policy that would reduce my chances of dying by 50 percent this next year." Authentic relationships are lifesavers.

But it doesn't stop with our bodies. Our need for community is stamped on our souls. We crave connection because we were not only created for community but also *from* community. It's the most perfect community that ever existed—the Father, Son, and Holy Spirit. So deep is their mutual love for one another, so profound their union, that they can actually be called the three in one, the Trinity, the triune God. Jesus described it this way: "The Father is in me and I am in the Father."[6]

Author and pastor John Ortberg notes, "The ancient Greek for this 'mutual indwelling' of the Trinity is *perichoresis*, which is related to our word *choreography*. The Trinity exists as a kind of eternal dance of joyful love among Father, Son, and Spirit."[7]

Our very bodies and souls are choreographed for community. When God sees lonely people, God still says, "Not good." In fact, God took this community idea to a whole new level. Out of great love, God sent Jesus to call us out of our lonely world and invite us into a new community—a spiritual family where we can be known, accepted, and encouraged to become all God intended. A beautiful picture of that new community is painted in the Bible in the second chapter of Acts.

> They devoted themselves to the apostles' teaching and to fellowship, to the breaking of bread and to prayer. . . . Every day they continued to meet together in the temple courts. They broke bread in their homes and ate together with glad and sincere hearts. . . . And the Lord added to their number daily those who were being saved.[8]

Here we catch a glimpse of God's original blueprint for the church. There's a powerful interplay between the large group who met in the temple courts and small groups who met in each other's homes. Years later, when the Apostle Paul was saying goodbye to the elders of the church in Ephesus, he encouraged them, "You know I held back nothing that would be helpful so that I could proclaim to you and teach you both publicly and privately in your homes."[9]

Here's the pattern again: meeting for teaching publically with a large group and in homes privately with a small group. Each setting is unique. Large group is designed for inspiration and instruction. It ushers us into the greatness of God. Small group sets the table for intimacy. It's where we experience the closeness of God. This dual design has been called God's 20/20 vision for the church.

A New Picture

But in most cases, it's not the vision people carry in their heads. Play along with me for a moment. When someone says the word *church*, what's the first image that pops in your mind?

It may be a big stone cathedral in a city or a white clapboard chapel in the country. It could be a large group of people on a Sunday morning or a TV preacher that goes on and on.

What if that image was something totally different? What if you heard the word *church* and the first picture that flashed in your mind was a group of ten people who get together at Jim and Jessica's house on Thursday nights at 7, or four guys who gather at a restaurant on Tuesday mornings at 6:30? What if the most important part of church is what happens when you are with a few other people trying to figure what it means to live like Jesus this week?

That idea had never occurred to me. I grew up in a very traditional church, sensed a call from God to become a pastor, and in the 1980s attended a seminary that provided an excellent education for managing the slow decline of a small to medium-sized church stuck in the 1950s, '60s, or '70s. For my first couple of years out of seminary, I was fine with that. God then infused me with a new dream: to start a new church. I didn't know the first thing about church planting or anyone who had done it successfully, but week by week, I felt a deeper calling to this kind of work. In 1991, I signed up for a conference called "How to Plant a Church." My hope was to pick up some basic ideas about how to get started. What I received was a completely new vision of how to do church. Among the major paradigm shifts of this "new community" was the way Jim Dethmer spoke of the small group system. He said, "All churches have small groups— Sunday school classes, the choir, the board, a prayer group. What I am describing is not a church that has small groups. It's a church that *is* small groups. It's a church made up of a bunch of small groups that gather every week for a large group worship celebration."[10]

That single thought changed the picture in my head. For the first time, my image of *church* shifted from large group to small, from Sunday morning worship to somebody's living room. The idea captivated me. I thought, "Someday, I'd like to be part of a church like that."

Imagine my surprise when I discovered John Wesley made this mental shift over 250 years earlier! Through the close fellowship of his small group, Wesley felt his heart "strangely warmed." His newfound assurance of faith in 1738 changed the compass in his spiritual life. True north was now the grace of God received by faith. He was no longer one of the Goodpeople, trusting in his good works and ethical behavior to earn him salvation. Wesley's experience of grace was so profound, he wanted everyone to taste this transforming love of God. His new vision was breathtaking in scope: "To reform the nation, and in particular the Church, and to spread scriptural holiness over the land."[11] Not surprisingly, Wesley chose to tackle this big goal primarily through small groups. But to the people of that day, his vision must have looked like a moon shot.

Holy Reform, Batman!

Holiness would not be the first word to describe the conditions of eighteenth-century England, nor the last. The Industrial Revolution was disrupting a centuries-old agrarian society. Newly emerging sea trade created a huge demand for manufactured goods. People were moving in droves from small farming communities to big cities to work in the newly built factories and mills. They arrived penniless, uprooted from their families, and divorced from long-held cultural traditions. Struggling to make sense of their new world, they often fell into evils rampant in the city slums. Children of the new working class were particularly vulnerable. To help their families, many were doing hard labor in coal mines or brickyards at the age of four or five. Less than one in twenty-five children received any formal education.[12]

Amid all the change, the most destructive force plowing through the working poor and their children was alcoholism. "In 1736 every sixth house in London was licensed as a grogshop [a drinking place of corrupt character]. Gin consumption topped eleven million gallons a year in England alone. This epidemic of drunkenness eroded what little decency was left among working people, leaving them adrift in hopeless despair."[13]

The wealthy aristocracy paid little attention to the plight of the poor. As their coffers increased on the backs of faceless laborers, they busied themselves with art, politics, trade, and polite living. The Church of England was just as oblivious, since it catered to the upper class. The clergy generally embraced deism, a belief in a distant God who has little involvement in people's lives or the affairs of this world. Since their salaries were paid by state taxes, they felt no obligation to their congregations. Their concern for the souls of their people was minimal. When it came to working class folk, their concern was nonexistent. The ruling class carefully controlled all aspects of religious expression. Worship services were highly regulated and routine for fear that someone might get "enthusiastic" and stir the unwashed masses into rebellion, as the Puritans did a century earlier.[14] Greed, apathy, and fear had left the church spiritually dead.

This was the nation and the church Wesley wanted to reform. Any takers? How on earth could holiness be spread in these conditions? Wesley accomplished his goal by following certain practices. First, he stayed close to the power of God in prayer, spending two hours a day in this holy exercise. Second, he chose to go to non-churched people and meet them on their turf and their terms. Third, he learned how to speak the language of the common people. Fourth, he found a way to tune into their hearts through music indigenous to their culture. Fifth, he discovered a way to help people do life together that would change both their heart and their behavior. Wesley created an interconnected system of groups tailored to a person's spiritual state and desire to grow. It revolved around the society and the class meeting.

Life Together

When Wesley began preaching outdoors, many people were "awakened" to their spiritual state and came to him for further help. He first organized them into "societies" of fifty or more. We would call them congregations. Here's how Wesley defined them: "Such a Society is no other than 'a company of men "having the form, and seeking the power of godliness", united in order to pray together, to receive the word of exhortation, and to watch over one another in love, that they may help each other to work out their salvation.'"[15]

The primary purpose of the society was instruction in the faith. The group would meet at various times during the week to hear a prepared talk about some aspect of Christian living. They sat in rows of backless benches, men on one side, women on the other. During the meetings, they would sing hymns, read scriptures, and have public prayer, but there was no provision for discussion. The society was for cognitive learning.[16]

Wesley soon found a flaw in this arrangement—too little spiritual oversight. Although learning is an essential part of life as a disciple, Wesley knew from his Oxford days that information by itself changes no one. Instruction has to be internalized for it to change the way a person lives. This took time and personal attention. As the movement grew, Wesley's inability to provide close pastoral supervision, especially to new converts, plagued him. He knew how easily people could slip back into a former way of life, but there simply wasn't enough of him to meet individually with the hundreds and then thousands of people responding to his preaching. His solution was the class meeting.

Wesley subdivided every society into classes of ten to twelve people that would meet weekly "to work out [their] own salvation."[17] He handpicked seasoned lay leaders to give pastoral oversight to each class and report the spiritual progress of each member. The term *class* was a misnomer. They were not organized for instruction. The goal was behavioral change. It was to apply what people had already learned in the society.[18]

Wesley envisioned each person seeking after personal holiness, a deep love of God and neighbor, "without which no one would see the Lord."[19] The weekly meetings focused on one's personal experience of God and honest sharing of struggles. The leader would begin by giving an account of his or her own journey of faith over the past week. Successes were shared along with failures, temptations, sins, and inner struggles. Once the leader set the pattern, class members would share in turn what God was doing in their lives.[20] The class meeting created a safe place to celebrate victories, share struggles, and confess sin. As a result, people were genuinely freed from guilt and propelled forward in their spiritual growth.

To guide their pursuit of holiness, Wesley created three "General Rules" for all involved in the societies: (1) do no harm, (2) do good, and (3) attend to spiritual disciplines that grow one's love for God. Each rule included specific behavioral goals that clearly defined what was in and out of bounds. Class members were to avoid such things as brawling, quarreling, drunkenness, taking the Lord's name in vain, and borrowing with no intention of paying back. They were encouraged to give food to the hungry, care for the sick, visit those in prison, and verbally share their faith. Wesley also recommended spiritual practices to strengthen their faith like public worship, family and private prayer, scripture reading, and fasting or abstinence.[21]

As people participated in this spiritual process, thousands of lives were radically changed. To pour fuel on this fire, Wesley made active participation in a class the condition for membership. To join a society, a person had to first spend three months in weekly class meetings. Once joined, persons could miss some of the large group society meetings, but if they missed more than three class meetings in a quarter, they could no longer be members of the society.[22] The message was clear: real church happened in the small group classes.

Wesley saw so much life change take place in these classes and so little fruit borne among those who didn't join one that he soon refused to preach in a place unless he could organize class meetings afterward. Awakening people to their true condition before God without offering them a safe place to learn the ways of God, wrote Wesley in his journal, "is only begetting children for the murderer." Their latter state would be worse than their former.[23]

Accordingly, Wesley made it as easy as possible to jump into a class. Social standing or spiritual pedigree meant nothing. The only requirement was a desire "to flee from the wrath to come, and to be saved from their sins."[24] In other words, a person must want to live a new life. The class meeting was where people could taste the warm fellowship, share their own struggles and sin, and come to faith in their true redeemer. Wesley knew real transformation didn't happen in an instant; it occurred over time. The journals of early Methodists bore this out. Many of them spent two to three years in weekly class meetings before they converted to Christ.

The Missing Piece

For most of us, this is a picture of church we have never seen. Growing up in twentieth-century Methodism, I believed the best way to grow as a Christian was to participate in a large group experience and do daily devotions. I thought, "If I can just make it to worship every week and have a personal devotional time each day, I'll really be knocking it out of the park." But as valuable as those practices are, something was missing. To discover who God made me to be, I needed a small group.

It was in my high school Sunday school class that someone first urged me to invite Jesus into my heart. My teacher, Sharon Rust, kept gently insisting that Christianity is not simply a relationship with the church; it's a relationship with Jesus Christ. Because of her witness and the support of that group, one day as a fourteen-year-old freshman I decided to invite Jesus into my heart for real. My life has never been the same.

In college, I was in a singing group that led worship services around central Illinois on Sundays. In that group of ten college students, I was loved, nurtured, and discipled in the faith. Through them I heard a whisper from God to leave behind my boyhood aspiration to be a marine biologist and instead become a pastor.

As I was studying for the ministry, I took a class on the New Testament book of Romans. Near the end of the semester, I was presenting a huge research paper to about a dozen classmates when time stood still. An eerie feeling came over me that they were really listening. Some took notes. Others put down their pens and stared at me. I thought something was stuck in my teeth. Afterward, one of them said, "Wow! That was really good, Roger." Another one said something similar. And then another. It caught us all off guard. What they affirmed that day was a spiritual gift I didn't know I had—the gift of teaching.

Apart from these groups, I may have never crossed the line of faith and become a Christian. I certainly would not have gone the pastor route and would have never received or understood the spiritual gifts God has given me to use for God's purpose. If it wasn't for a group of Christian friends, I would have never met my wife, Leanne. Our kids, Zach and Jane, would have never been born. My whole life would be different if I had not decided to do life together with a few other people.

Scripture says, "So if anyone is in Christ, there is a new creation: everything old has passed away; see, everything has become new!"[25] A friend of mine used to say, "SEE? See how you are?" In every stage of my life, I've needed a group of people to help me see who I really am in Christ.

Wesley saw what many Christians miss today—the inadequacy of a church whose only focus is the large group. Instruction without application leads to arrogance. "Knowledge puffs up," says Paul, "but love builds up."[26] It is not what you know; it's how you love that counts. Most of us are educated well beyond the level of our obedience. We need a safe place where we can ask our questions, share our struggles, and internalize what we have been taught. Without someplace to process our faith, it never becomes real.

A Safe Place

Emmaus Group

Where is your safe place?

Do you have a handful of people you meet with regularly who will allow you to pull down the mask and say, "Look, here's who I am. This is what keeps me up at night. This is where I'm falling short. Here's what God is calling me to do, but I don't have the guts to do it. This is the image I project, but underneath, it's not that good"?

In a hyperconnected world, most of us don't need more relationships. We need deeper ones. Do you have a safe place where faith can become real?

Author Gordon MacDonald told about visiting a small group of men and women affiliated with Alcoholics Anonymous. MacDonald said he visited the group because he has friends who are recovering alcoholics, and he wanted to see for himself what they were talking about. Here's what he found:

> One morning Kathy—I guessed her age at 35—joined us for the first time. One look at her face caused me to conclude that she must have been Hollywood-beautiful at 21. Now her face was swollen, her eyes red, her teeth rotting. Her hair looked unwashed, uncombed for who knows how long.
>
> "I've been in five states in the past month," she said. "I've slept under bridges on several nights. Been arrested. Raped. Robbed (now weeping). I don't know what to do. I . . . don't . . . want . . . to . . . be . . . homeless . . . any more. But (sob) I can't stop drinking (sob). I can't stop (sob). I can't. . . ."
>
> Next to Kathy was a rather large woman, Marilyn, sober for more than a dozen years. She reached with both arms toward Kathy and pulled her close, so close that Kathy's face was pressed to Marilyn's ample breast. I was close enough to hear Marilyn speak quietly into Kathy's ear, "Honey, you're going to be OK. You're with us now. We can deal with this together. All you have to do is keep coming. Hear me? Keep on coming." And then Marilyn kissed the top of Kathy's head.[27]

That's a safe place. It mirrors the kind of authentic community the Methodist class meetings were known for. No wonder they grew so rapidly. Wesley knew from his own experience that people cannot change until they are accepted just as they are. Once they taste that kind of acceptance, all they have to do is keep on coming, and they will be loved to a new life.

Are there safe places in your church where people can be loved to life? The Christian faith has always been more caught than taught. To catch it a person has to hang around others that are contagious. Does your group or church have a process of discipleship that includes nonchurched people, leads them to faith, and grows them into mature followers of Christ?

Close the Gap

Most churches have large group worship experiences that provide good instruction, perhaps even inspiration for Christian living. Leaders typically spend an inordinate amount of time and resources on their weekly worship celebration. On the whole, the focus is heavily weighted on cognitive learning. Services often feel like a college course where as much information as possible is crammed into listeners' brains. But with no place to process that information, it has little effect on daily living. This explains how some people can sit in church week after week for decades and show no more evidence of Christ's love, joy, or peace than the day they first attended. By itself, large group worship creates an ever-widening gap between what people know and what they actually do.

Small groups close the gap. Real, lasting life change does not happen when someone is sitting in an auditorium listening to a talking head. It happens when a person is in a room with a handful of others and someone asks, "What is God doing in your life this week? Where are you struggling? How can we pray for you?" People don't grow in rows. They grow in circles.

Just ask Taisia. Remember her prayer on the way to church? All she wanted was one friend.

> Little did I know how richly God would answer me. It was truly ten-fold. I never really understood what the phrases *church family* or *brothers and sisters in Christ* meant. I thought that was just something polite people in church said. It's become so completely clear to me now. That's truly the way it feels. I may be five hundred miles away from my biological family, but I have a family here now. We'll be together to celebrate successes and to mourn each other's losses. Before I found a group, my faith felt self-satisfying and incredibly private. Now it's more of an outpouring. It's more generous and vibrant. I've found my tribe and my walk with Christ is much more whole.

Taisia discovered the double bonus of authentic community. It not only satisfies the deep longing in our souls to be connected but also fosters spiritual transformation of heart and life. In community, our faith turns into an outpouring of our lives for others.

Prayer

Lord Jesus, you know how lonely this life can be. Help me find a few other people who can become a safe place for me. Use them to close the gap in my life and show me who I am in you.

Hiding God's Word in my Heart

Every day they continued to meet together in the temple courts. They broke bread in their homes and ate together with glad and sincere hearts . . . And the Lord added to their number daily those who were being saved.

—Acts 2:46-47 (NIV)

Discussion guide available at www.MeetTheGoodpeople.com.

Get Everyone in the Game

The meaning of life is service to others.

—Dallas Willard

The Spirit's presence is shown in some way in each person for the good of all.

—1 Corinthians 12:7 (GNT)

C hristie grew up in the church. Her parents were actively involved in their faith and wanted the same for their children. Her earliest memories revolve around attending Sunday school and worship with her family, going to Vacation Bible School in the summer, and playing Joseph in the Christmas play. (They couldn't get a boy to wear the robe that year.) When she was old enough, she couldn't wait to join her church's youth group. Christie loved church—it was her extended family. The only thing that didn't add up was the faith part. She knew the rules and did her best to follow them. She was cheerful, respectful, and responsible—a model child. What no one knew was how empty she felt on the inside. Afraid of what others might think, she kept her feelings to herself, hoping someday it would all make sense.

The summer before her senior year, Christie's youth group took a mission trip to build Habitat for Humanity houses in a neighboring state. High school students and adult sponsors piled into fifteen-passenger vans to make the twelve-hour drive to the site. They worked in ninety-five-degree heat hanging drywall, mudding seams, putting in insulation, and digging culverts. It was hard, sweaty work. At times, the group worked alongside the eventual homeowners, who put in their own "sweat equity." At night, the group would go to a church basement to eat a good meal, have group devotions, and play games. At the end of the week, everyone came back tired, slaphappy, and carrying an odd sense of peace.

Months later, someone noticed a difference in Christie's life. Her smile was more genuine; her personality more at ease. When asked about it, she said, "I became a Christian. It happened on the mission trip." Seeing the confused look on her friend's face, she explained. "It was Saturday during the long ride home. Most of the people around me were asleep. With no one to talk to, I began thinking about all the things we did. 'People we didn't even know before this week will now have a home for the very first time,' I thought. 'They were so happy . . . I guess because God did something for them that they couldn't do for themselves.' Suddenly, a warm feeling came over me, and it clicked: 'This is what it means to be a Christian. Jesus did something for me that I couldn't do for myself. He forgave me and gave me a new home in heaven. It's not about how good I am. It's about loving others the way Jesus loved me.' It was so clear. I knew that's what I really wanted, so I turned my life over to Jesus right in the middle of the van."

We usually focus on people getting the right beliefs and assume the behavior will follow. It also works the opposite way. New behaviors can lead to deep changes in belief. Christie's radiant, new faith was a testimony to the transforming power of serving.

Upside Down

Serving changes us because it draws us to the heart of God. Jesus knew this implicitly. From the start, his public ministry was filled with brilliant teaching, astonishing healings, and jaw-dropping miracles. His fame soon preceded him. When he entered an area, crowds would gather by the thousands. Experiencing such hope in him, people often tried to make him their earthly king, but each time Jesus refused. It was not why he came.

Jesus desperately wanted his followers to be clear about his larger mission. Unfortunately, they made it about themselves. At one point, his disciples had a selfishness eruption. Two of them secretly tried to secure the top spots in Jesus's kingdom. When the other ten heard about it, they were outraged. Hard chunks of resentment began to form. Realizing the offense was severe enough to split the group, Jesus turned it into the perfect teaching moment.

He called them together and said, "Look, guys, you think this is about climbing to the top of the organizational chart and lording power and authority over people. It's not. If you want to be great, be a servant. To follow me, the first among you must be slave of all."[1]

He then revealed his true identity. "For even the Son of Man did not come to be served; he came to serve and to give his life to redeem many people."[2] The silence among them must have been deafening. No leader had ever said anything like that before. Jesus came to establish an upside-down kingdom where the greatest are the least. To follow him means to take on a new identity—that of a servant. You might wonder why Jesus invites people prone to selfish eruptions to become slaves of all. Frankly, he knows how we are made.

Shellfish

American educator Laurence Peter wrote, "There are two kinds of egotists: Those who admit it, and the rest of us."[3] We knowingly smile at that quote, but at times we still struggle to see ourselves in that latter category.

A little girl was being selfish to her brothers. Finally, her dad sat her down and gave her a long lecture about being selfish.

When he was done, the little girl said, "Daddy, I don't even have a shellfish!"

Helping people see their selfishness is like trying to get a shellfish to see water. There's something about our nature that is immersed in itself. Of course, someone might say, "Yeah, I can be selfish. What difference does it make?"

Actually, quite a lot.

In a major study from Duke University, 1,037 persons were followed from childhood to age thirty-two. Researchers were trying to measure the "executive function" that allows us to exert control over our thoughts and impulses. Basically, it keeps us from selfishly grabbing whatever we want whenever we want.

The results were sobering. "Children followed from birth to age 32 who could better regulate their impulses and attention were four times less likely to have a criminal record, three times less likely to be addicted to drugs and half as likely to become single parents."[4]

The study also discovered a number of long-term, negative consequences to selfishness in adults.

- Inability to give to maintain a successful loving relationship
- A life of loneliness and severe sadness
- Excessive anger which harms relationships
- Treatment of others as objects to be used and not as persons
- Failure to care for children or spouse
- Substance abuse
- Financial irresponsibility
- Lack of faith[5]

Left to ourselves, this is what we become. Selfishness destroys us. The question is how to escape it. Some would say through willpower. We must simply choose to focus on others. Unfortunately, we're too immersed in ourselves to do that consistently. Theologian W. Paul Jones describes our dilemma this way: "The selfish cannot will to be selfless."[6] Our nature is so self-centered that the only way we could choose a selfless life is if there is something in it for us. Ironically, willpower is powerless to change our most basic need. It can't change our "self" from the inside out.

That kind of alteration requires help from the outside. Jesus came to deliver us from our selfish disregard for God and others. On the cross he willingly paid in blood the penalty for our selfishness—he died for us. When we apply his forgiving love to our lives by faith, it does for us what our willpower could never do. It changes the composition of our hearts. We are forgiven for our selfish pursuits and freed for selfless service. Over time the Holy Spirit transforms our corrupted core to a Christlike one. This is how the Goodpeople become God's people.

Saved to Serve

The Apostle Paul talks about it this way: "For by grace you have been saved through faith, and this is not your own doing; it is the gift of God—not the result of works, so that no one may boast. For we are what he has made us, created in Christ Jesus for good works, which God prepared beforehand to be our way of life."[7]

We have been saved to serve. Maybe you have wondered why God didn't take you to heaven the second you accepted Jesus's forgiveness by faith and became a Christian. Why didn't God save you from all the heartache and troubles of this world and take you straight into eternal bliss?

There is a reason you're still here: to do the good works God has prepared beforehand to be your way of life. It's your purpose. God has prepared both small tasks and large ones for you. Your job is to keep your eyes open for the serving adventures God has arranged in advance.

We all want to know what adventures God has in store. One night I was putting to bed our then seven-year-old daughter, Jane. Instead of reading a book, we decided to turn out all the lights, close the door, and look up at the stars—the little plastic stars on her ceiling that glowed in the dark. In a few moments, we started seeing different shapes. "Look," she said, "that one looks like a deer with antlers." "See that one?" I said. "It looks like the Big Dipper."

Our stargazing went on for a while until it got quiet. Just when I thought she was nodding off, Janie turned toward me and said, "Daddy, what do you think I am going to be?"

It was a tender moment. Fortunately, I had already thought about this. I said softly, "You are going to be something special, Honey. God has something very special for you to do." That was enough for her. To be honest, I don't know exactly what that is, but I know it is true. It is true about you, too.

The Power of Everyone

God has something special for you to do. God created you to be a spiritual leader, but there's no need to rush out and buy a clergy collar just yet. In the time before Christ, God chose a few people to be the spiritual leaders of God's people, the Israelites. These were the

65

priests. They were "marked by special training, a special garb, a special vocabulary and a special way of life."[8] Their special function was to lead the religious ceremonies, pray the formal prayers, and make the atonement for sins on behalf of the people. At that time, if there was anything religious to be done, the priest led or oversaw it. They were the "go-betweens" who connected the people with God.

But that all changed when Christ came. Jesus ushered in a new era for those who would be his followers. Peter, a common fisherman who became the leader of Jesus's disciples, describes this new way of life in a letter to everyday Christ followers. "But you are a chosen race, a royal priesthood, a holy nation, a people who are God's own possession. You have become this people so that you may speak of the wonderful acts of the one who called you out of darkness into his amazing light."[9]

This passage makes some people break out in hives. "Wait a minute," you might say. "I can't be a priest. I'm not qualified." The crazy thing about this new era is it doesn't matter. God doesn't call the qualified. God qualifies the called. Apparently, having a real relationship with Jesus is enough to get started.

Many pastors and laypeople are still trying to wrap their minds around this one. When I first began serving as a pastor, I discovered I had a special function to perform. The congregations I served needed someone to pray before official spiritual events like volleyball games, hog roasts, and board meetings. It was my job to preach, baptize, visit the sick, bury the dead, marry the willing, teach the youth, evangelize the wayward, counsel the troubled, help the poor, and hold the hand of those in personal crisis. That was too much to keep in mind all at once, so in my head I shortened the list to three: hatch, match, and dispatch. Of course, the members also had a job—to attend and give some money.

When I realized the unwritten job descriptions, I thought, "No wonder I'm so tired!" It was a direct throwback to Old Testament times. In the view of those congregations, the pastor and maybe a few staff people were the "priests." It was their job to do all the spiritual stuff because they have a special relationship with God that the rest of the congregation didn't have. "It's the minister's job," they would say. "We're not qualified."

In their defense, it seems that no one had ever taught them this truth out of scripture called *the priesthood of all believers*. In a nutshell, it means every follower of Christ is a minister of Christ. Every member of the body is a minister in the body. What qualifies someone for ministry is a person's relationship with Jesus, not a seminary degree. Jesus said, "You didn't choose me, but I chose you and appointed you so that you could go and produce fruit and so that your fruit could last."[10]

Christianity was never designed to be spectator sport. There is no bench warming. You have been chosen to play on the team, and Jesus has a position in mind for every one of his followers.

As the eighteenth-century revival took off, Wesley rediscovered this ancient truth and harnessed its power for spiritual growth. With the early Methodist movement doubling in size each year, Wesley soon took his mother's advice and allowed laypersons, both men and women, to oversee the small group class meetings and preach in the large group society meetings. He took a boatload of criticism for opening the doors of ministry to people who were not properly educated and credentialed by the Church of England. Some of it came from his brother, Charles. Regardless, Wesley came up with his own credentialing process. In addition to asking if they knew a pardoning God and had gifts for the work, Wesley wanted to know, "Have they fruit?"[11] In other words, has their faith in Christ produced changed lives for Christ? If so, that was evidence of their readiness for ministry. Further education and mentoring could take place in the trenches. Wesley's concern was to get as many spiritually qualified people as possible "on the field" to give spiritual oversight to newly awakened explorers and newly born Christians. When he released the energies of the laity, the ministry multiplied even faster.

Commissioning people to serve carried a double bonus. It not only fueled the movement but also touched the needs of each person's soul. Wesley discovered this reality early on. As a young man, he was influenced by the life and writings of a Catholic nobleman, Monr. de Renty (1611–1649).[12] At twenty-seven, de Renty had such a vivid experience of Christ, he devoted the rest of his life to caring for the poor and establishing small societies for those who earnestly sought a holy life.[13] The societies de Renty established in his native country of France were similar to the religious societies Wesley knew so well in England nearly a century later. There was just one significant difference. The Anglican societies assumed serving others would be the ultimate *result* of their spiritual growth. For de Renty, service to others was a *pathway* for spiritual growth.[14] Early on, Wesley sided

with de Renty and encoded in Methodism's DNA a deep conviction that ministering to the needs of others is a means of receiving
God's transforming grace. He called such service "works of mercy"
and strongly encouraged the Methodist people to engage in these
works as a way to grow in holiness.

Getting Everyone in the Game

Holiness is directly connected to loving others. As Rick Warren
said in the classic first line of his book *The Purpose Driven Life*, "It's
not about you."[15] It's a phrase I need to hear daily. Left to ourselves,
we're like the little girl who can't see that she is "shellfish." To help
everyday people move from "serve us" to "service," here's a three-part
process any group or church can use.

1. Teach about Servanthood and Spiritual Gifts

When I moved to Springfield, the first extended message series
we did was about serving. For several weeks that fall we laid the biblical foundation for following Jesus as one who serves. Here are some
of the core truths we shared.

> To jumpstart a flat-lined faith, pray a dangerous prayer: "Use
> me."
>
> The number of people on the planet: seven billion; the number
> of God's "burning bushes" available: one a piece.
>
> Every follower of Christ is a minister of Christ.
>
> We grow in Christ by serving others.
>
> Every believer in Christ has at least one spiritual gift to be
> discovered, deployed, and developed.

To have a greater impact, our weekly worship services included
in-person or video testimonies of church members describing their
joy in serving. We also encouraged small groups and Sunday school
classes to use a study guide on the joy of serving, so people would
have a place to internalize what they were being taught.

2. *Help People Discover Their Spiritual Gifts*

Most people have no idea how committed God is to serving. I sure didn't. Not only did God send Jesus to save us from our selfishness, re-create us in Christ to serve others, and prepare in advance good works for us to do, God also gives every believer in Christ special abilities to carry out that service. By faith in Christ, we are saved to serve through God-given spiritual gifts.

This was a revelation to me. I grew up in the church, attended a church-related college, invested in four years of seminary, and never heard anything about God's personalized plan for serving. Only later did I discover that as a follower of Christ, I had been given gifts to serve others. I found that a spiritual gift is a supernatural ability God gives to each Christ follower to advance God's purposes. Scripture describes it this way: "There are different kinds of spiritual gifts, but the same Spirit gives them. . . .There are different abilities to perform service, but the same God gives ability to all for their particular service. The Spirit's presence is shown in some way in each person for the good of all."[16]

A full discussion of spiritual gifts is beyond the scope of this book. For now, here's a snapshot of how they work. Each believer in Christ has been given by the Spirit at least one spiritual gift and possibly a cluster of three or four. Each gift is an attribute of Jesus. While on earth, Jesus demonstrated all the gifts—mercy, evangelism, teaching, healing, leadership, hospitality, serving, and a host of others.[17] Now that Jesus is no longer here physically, God distributes one or more of these gifts to every Christ follower so that we may serve one another.[18] No one has all the gifts, but every member of the body has at least one. That's why we need each other.[19]

Each believer is a vital organ in Christ's body.[20] Just as your body cannot fully function if it's missing a lung or the kidneys are not working, so the body of Christ cannot function at its full capacity without you discovering and deploying your unique gifts!

Most of us need help to uncover our gifts. During the message series mentioned above, we invited people to a two-hour class on Saturday morning called "Discover Your Spiritual Gifts." A series of Sunday school classes or small group meetings are also great settings to look at the scripture passages on spiritual gifts, discuss how they work in the body, and take a spiritual gift inventory to identify possible gifts. Often the best way to discover a gift is to ask the people in our small group or class. When we do life with a handful of people over time, they may see a gift working in our lives before we do.

3. Help People Deploy Their Spiritual Gifts

Once people get an inkling of their gifts, they need some guidance to put them into play. Creating a menu of serving opportunities in the church is a great place to start. It's best if those serving opportunities are listed under the spiritual gift associated with that activity. For instance, hospital visits would be under the gift of mercy, ushers and greeters would be under the gift of hospitality, and so on. If you hope to involve people who have never served, a handy on-ramp is "First Serve" opportunities. These initial, short-term experiences in a particular ministry give people a chance to get their feet wet. Trying a First Serve is a great way to see if that ministry is a good fit. If not, the person can try a different First Serve.

The whole process works best when a shepherd guides it. We invite persons with the gift of discernment or shepherding to help people match their spiritual gifts with the best place to serve. Our shepherds receive training to help people through the gift-discovery process and find their sweet spot of serving. Since people rarely find their sweet spot on the first try, our shepherds suggest other opportunities and encourage them to stick with it until they find their perfect fit. If no fit can be found, it may be a sign to create a new ministry that aligns with that person's gifts, personality, and heart passion.

By this point you have probably noticed the 180-degree shift that's taken place. A gift-based approach to ministry focuses on the need of the individual to serve rather than the need of the institution to be served. Most people these days don't care much about filling a church's institutional slots. They simply want to know if God is real, if God cares about them, and if their lives have some greater purpose. The best way to help them personally embrace these realities is through a serving opportunity that fits the way God wired them.

Recent research surveying 250,000 members and attenders across one thousand churches of every size and spiritual heritage revealed that "serving is the most catalytic experience offered by the church."[21] It produces spiritual growth in all stages of a person's spiritual journey, from spiritual explorer to Christ-centered believer. In fact, serving has a greater impact on spiritual growth than organized small groups or weekend worship services.[22]

What would it be like if we set aside the slots, sat down with someone and said, "Who has God made you to be?" Imagine the dreams of God that could be released. With an individual approach rather than an institutional one, we don't have to arm twist anyone into serving. We just turn people loose. The Spirit knows better than we do the gifts needed for Christ's body.

That's what Tim discovered. Serving as a shepherd, he sat down with Justin after work one day to talk about where this thirty-year-old husband, father, and engineer might want to serve. When Tim casually asked, "How long have you been a Christian?" Justin said, "We need to talk about that."

Justin could not really pinpoint a time; he'd been in and out of church a lot. As they talked, Tim explained the basics of the gospel and Justin expressed a desire to know Christ personally. When Tim asked him if he would like to pray a prayer of surrender, Justin said, "Yes, I would."

What followed was a moment neither of them will forget. "He wept, and I wept," Tim said. "He thanked me a number of times, and I thanked him for the gift of leading him across the starting line. He and I are going to read the Gospel of John together and discuss it over the next couple of weeks."

When I heard that story, I shook my head in amazement. Justin went on to discover his gifts and is now a fantastic servant in the church. He's in the game all the time and serves with sheer joy. Every time I see him, I smile. That's what serving through spiritual gifts can do. Imagine the possibilities if this kind of thing were to go viral.

Prayer
Lord, use me.

Hiding God's Word in My Heart
For we are what he has made us, created in Christ Jesus for good works, which God prepared beforehand to be our way of life.

—Ephesians 2:10

Discussion guide available at www.MeetTheGoodpeople.com.

Go Global

I look upon all the world as my parish.

—John Wesley

I t's a line from a letter. It was John's response to the severe criticism he received from Josiah Tucker, the directing pastor of All Saints Church in Bristol. By 1739, just a year after his heartwarming experience on Aldersgate Street, both Wesley and his young friend, George Whitefield, had been banned from preaching in nearly every Anglican church in Britain. Their enthusiastic message of salvation by faith was too much for the staid Church of England. Undeterred, they left the buildings and went to the people. The response was staggering. As they preached outdoors on hillsides or the market square, anywhere from three thousand to seventeen thousand people crowded in to hear the gospel. Wesley quickly organized the spiritually awakened into societies of a few dozen each, as well as smaller groups that would band together for prayer and mutual accountability.[1]

Rev. Tucker's gripe was that Wesley and Whitefield were acting illegally.[2] At the time, England was divided into parishes, small geographical areas akin to counties in the United States. Each parish had a parish church. Everyone living within the bounds of a parish belonged to its church, and clergy were strictly forbidden from "sheep stealing" in someone else's parish. In Tucker's mind, both of these men were clearly breaking the rules. Wesley's response to both Tucker and the bishop of Bristol, Joseph Butler, later became a rallying cry of Methodism.

In his letter, Wesley explained that God had called him to preach. As a lecturer and tutor at Oxford College, he was not ordained to a specific parish, but to the whole of the Church of England. Therefore, he wrote, "I look upon all the world as my parish."[3]

As the revival spread faster and farther, those words took on much greater significance. *The world is my parish* is now a watchword of Wesleyan Christians all around the globe. It captures the missionary mindset of Methodism from its inception, and it reflects God's world-saving mission in Jesus. Like Wesley, if we're willing to be led by the Spirit, we too can go global. It's never been easier.

A Whole New World

We live in an unparalleled time. The Internet and social media enable anyone with web access to have a personal platform previously unimaginable. To get a sense of scale, take a look at the three most popular Twitter accounts in June 2015:

@katyperry: 71.41 million followers

@justinbieber: 64.92 million followers

@barackobama: 60.74 million followers[4]

In seconds, Katy Perry can send a personal message of 140 characters or less to 71 million of her closest friends all over the world. As you may know, Ms. Perry is not a head of state. She is not the CEO of a multinational corporation, nor does she run an international NGO. She's a pop star. Yet she can instantly and repeatedly connect with more people than the "leader of the free world." Of course, you may not care about sending messages that emphasize text. You may be a selfie queen or a photo czar who loves to share pictures. If so, you could take a cue from the 300 million people who have become active Instagram users since late 2010. This photo-sharing app allows its community "to connect to the world as it happens" through stills and videos that tell the story.[5] Afraid you might share too many pics? No worries. Instagram users share 70 million photos every day, which adds to the site's base of 30 billion pictures.[6]

No doubt some of you will want to connect on a larger scale. Perhaps you've heard of a little side project started in a college dorm room called Facemash. The world knows it by another name now. At latest count, Facebook has 1.44 billion active users and is growing—rapidly.[7] If it were a country, it would be the second most populated in the world, slightly behind China.[8] Founded in 2004, Facebook's mission is "to give people the power to share and make the world more open and connected."[9] To facilitate our desire for global sharing, Facebook makes 70 languages available—a necessity since 75 percent of all Facebook users are outside the United States.[10] Taken together, these stats give some sense of the magnitude of change the world is experiencing. But by the time you read this, the numbers will be so much higher you'll probably chuckle. We are witnessing a global phenomenon of social connection inconceivable in 2002, the year Facebook cofounder Mark Zuckerberg graduated from high school.

A Social Revolution

Our exponential connectedness has ushered us into a new era. Some years back, we left behind the Industrial Age and ran headlong into the Information Age. Now all those bytes of information are morphing into something profoundly new. Some have called it the *Social Age*.[11] What is it like to live in this new reality? Here are two sure signs of the social revolution.

1. Everyday People Find Their Voice

Previously in human history, you needed a platform of fame, fortune, military strength, or political power to effect change on a national or global level. Now all you need is a browser. Celebrities, billionaires, and star athletes no longer corner the market. Access to the Internet has leveled the playing field. In cyberspace, your link is no better or worse, no more or less important than anyone else's. Your ability to share ideas, sell a product, build a community, champion a cause, convey artistic beauty, or recruit an army are limited only by your ingenuity and persistence.

When unheard people finally find their voice, change is on the way. In recent years, we've seen entire governments toppled by Twitter. The Arab Spring of 2011 produced mass protests, demonstrations for democracy, and deposed dictators after decades of tyranny—all choreographed through tweets.[12] In the business world a similar dynamic is at play. Social media entrepreneurs say, "The balance of power has shifted from message-controlling corporations to customers and employees who can now voice their opinions—both good and bad—through social."[13]

One such power shift came just after Christmas in 2011. Verizon announced a two-dollar "convenience fee" for any customer who wanted to make a onetime online bill payment. Anyone could sign up for the regular online payments at no additional cost, but if you merely wanted to check your bill to be sure there were no unwarranted charges before paying it, you would have to pony up for the "convenience."[14]

The new policy rubbed more than a few people the wrong way. After the story broke early in the morning, it ballooned on Twitter throughout the day. By day's end, Verizon released a new statement. The proposed fee had been canceled. To their credit, Verizon's leaders heard the outcry, admitted it was a mistake, reversed their decision, and apologized—in less than one business day.[15] Beware the power of the Twittersphere.

Brianna Cotter of Change.org, a website devoted to changing the world through online activism, described the debacle this way: "Companies used to think they could get away with putting out unpopular policies. Today, hundreds of thousands of people can mobilize and change policies in a matter of hours. That's what we're seeing with Verizon."[16] People who once had little recourse as they faced oppressive governments, unfair business policies, or soulless bureaucracies can now let their voice be heard. And it's changing our world.

2. People Are Spontaneously Connected

Social media also connects people spontaneously, as Brandon discovered. All Brandon wanted to do was make his grandma happy. Given her circumstances, he figured the least he could do was pick up a bowl of her favorite soup. He had no idea it would get national attention. Here's how Brandon described it in a Facebook post.

> My grandmother is passing soon with cancer. I visited her the other day and she was telling me about how she really wanted soup, but not hospital soup because she said it tasted "awful"[;] she went on about how she really would like some clam chowder from Panera. Unfortunately Panera only sells clam

chowder on Friday. I called the manager, Sue, and told them the situation. I wasn't looking for anything special just a bowl of clam chowder. Without hesitation she said absolutely she would make her some clam chowder. When I went to pick up they wound up giving me a box of cookies as well. It's not that big of a deal to most, but to my grandma it meant a lot. I really want to thank Sue and the rest of the staff from Panera in Nashua NH just for making my grandmother happy.

Thank you so much![17]

To express her gratitude to this bakery-café chain, Brandon's mom shared the post on Panera's Facebook page. In just a few days, that short post received over half a million likes! At this point, that number has reached over eight hundred thousand. There have been nearly thirty-five thousand comments on the post praising Panera for that one act of kindness.[18]

When a magazine picked up the story, Brandon said, "If my grandma even knew what a Facebook page was, I'd show her . . . My grandma's biggest fear was dying with no friends. I wish I could show her how many 'friends' she has out there, and how many prayers people are saying for her."[19]

I ran across this story in a book designed for business people. The authors shared it to show how a single post could positively impact a national brand like Panera. What touched me was the human side of the storyline, the impact the post had on Brandon, and his mom, and, through the prayers of so many people, his grandma. The better part of a million people "liked" that story and were inspired by it. That's the power of social media. It connects people.

Fittingly, that business book, *A World Gone Social*, would have never been written apart from tweets. The authors, Ted Coiné and Mark Babbitt, live on opposite coasts in the United States. They met on Twitter. After the book came out, I heard about it on Twitter and bought a copy. Five years ago, I couldn't imagine a series of connections like that. Now, it's increasingly common.

When I asked my Facebook friends what they loved most about social media, by far the number one answer was "staying connected to friends and family." One woman shared with delight how she found a childhood friend on Facebook that she hadn't talked to in forty-five years. As I looked down the list of twenty-nine people that responded in the span of a few hours, I realized they represented eight different eras of my life. A little under half of them live far enough away that I rarely, if ever, see them face to face. We don't talk on the phone or text. Without Facebook, I would have no contact with them. With Facebook, I know what is happening in their lives. I can laugh at their sense of humor, pray for their struggles, and keep tabs on their kids. Though we no longer share life on a daily basis, we are still connected.

Of course, anything with the power to give people a voice and connect them on a worldwide scale can be used for good or for evil. The rise of ruthless terrorist groups is largely due to their sophisticated use of social media to gather new recruits. Our challenge as Christ followers is to be at least as intentional about unleashing social media to make disciples of Jesus.

Doorways to the World

In Wesley's day, the mass communication tool was the printing press. Wesley wrote numerous sermons, treatises, tracts, and books that were published and distributed to a wide audience to fuel the movement. Today Twitter, Facebook, YouTube, Instagram, Snapchat, blogs, and various other social media are doorways to over a billion people. Like never before, individual Christians have a staggering opportunity to "go into all the world" and share their faith. But to harness social media for the gospel, we have to understand how it works.

It's about Relationship

With potential access to a global audience, it's tempting to think of social media as a megaphone to the world. In reality, it's more like a memoir. It's not about shouting; it's about sharing. What drives the explosive growth of social media is our innate need to be known and understood. We want to tell our story, share our thoughts, compare experiences, and connect. It's about relationship. The goal is not to make a statement, but to invite someone into a conversation. Like a memoir, you may share touching or troubling events from your life. "Aha!" moments, hard losses, and turning points make for great posts, because they connect with a deep place in our souls.

Recently, a friend shared a sad anniversary on Facebook. He told of the tears he had shed that day over an unborn son he and his wife lost through a miscarriage nineteen years before. Although grateful for their other children, he spoke of the hopes they had and the ache they still feel for the son they never brought home. It was deeply personal. It was also freeing for many who felt drawn to console him. His unmasked grief acted as a release valve for others to share similar experiences. Those who felt trapped in a lonely place suddenly found they weren't alone. They had entered a community that understood. This is how social media works. It trades on a human truth: "The more personal, the more universal."[20]

The more personal our posts about faith, the more likely they will draw people into a conversation of redeeming value. Jesus told his disciples, "I don't call you servants . . . I call you friends."[21] Ministry has always traveled across the bridge of relationship. In the Social Age, that reality is multiplied many times over.

Engage

Most of us cut our teeth on broadcast media. We flip on the TV and watch it. We click on the car radio and listen. It's passive. The one-way flow of communication requires very little of us. We can pay attention or tune out. Many of us turn on a ball game as a sedative for a Sunday afternoon nap. Others use broadcast media to intentionally disengage from the world around them. How many people sit in front of a TV screen for hours each night to forget about the day and withdraw? Social media is a different kind of communication. It's an interactive, community conversation that encourages people to engage.

Adam Hamilton discovered the engaging nature of social media when he began using Facebook in 2006. Hamilton is the senior pastor of The United Methodist Church of the Resurrection in the greater Kansas City area, a megachurch of over eight thousand in average worship attendance. For him, Facebook is an indispensable way to connect and communicate with some thirty thousand "friends." Hamilton posts three to five times a week. Most are very short, but some are three paragraphs long. One of his favorite uses is what he calls "crowd-sourcing sermons."[22] The week before we spoke, he preached on Jesus as savior. On that Wednesday, he posted to his friends: "Tell me, how has Jesus saved you? What he saved you from, and what has he saved you to?" He clearly said he was looking for personal stories for that weekend's sermon, and he would probably pick two or three to share with the congregation. In a short time, he had forty-five to fifty comments, some deeply moving. A woman whose fourteen-year-old son had taken his own life in their home described how Jesus had saved her from the despair of that loss. There were people who felt Jesus had saved them from self-righteousness. Others talked about being saved from their addictions. Anyone who read the responses could be touched and inspired by these real-life stories. Hamilton ended up using six of them in his sermon and created a short video out of another eight to show during Holy Communion. He said, "It was a really powerful tool. I had stories from real, live people, many of whom are sitting in the pews on a given week. It was hugely helpful."[23]

In the Social Age, we don't just enjoy the experience; we also have the chance to shape it. I confess I'm a latecomer to the social media party. I was converted by both the connection with others and the level of engagement I experienced. It can be more personal than e-mail, but not as scary as a face-to-face talk. There's sometimes a confessional feel to it. But best of all, we get to be part of the conversation. In many cases, we help determine the outcome.

Jesus was a consummate engager. Take a look at the people in his life: smelly fisherman by the seashore, a Samaritan woman at a well, despised tax collectors, scorned prostitutes, self-righteous Pharisees, little children, blind men, Roman centurions, and unclean lepers, to name a few. You've got to admit, he had range. Through social media, we can follow his lead and extend our range by engaging in conversations we would likely never have any other way. For these conversations to be real, though, we must be willing to lose control.

Lose Control

You may have never heard of him. I hadn't. But due to the Internet and social media, he's the most famous whale in the South Pacific. Back in 2007, the Japanese government allowed limited humpback whaling in the Southern Ocean Whale Sanctuary. Greenpeace quickly opposed the decision and planned to use tracking chips to follow the movements of the massive mammals. To raise awareness, they decided to personify a whale through a naming campaign. The Internet poll offered thirty choices, including names from South

Pacific culture such as Aiko, Manami, and Kaimana. Also on the list was Mister Splashy Pants.[24]

One of these names went viral. Bloggers and social news websites such as Reddit, Fark, and BoingBoing strongly encouraged their followers to vote. As a result, Mister Splashy Pants went from 5 percent of the votes to about 70 percent in a day. It appeared there was a clear winner, but because some at Greenpeace were hoping for a more suitable name, they extended the voting for another week. This, of course, turned the naming contest into a quest. The Internet community banded around it. Facebook groups were created. "Vote your conscience, vote for Mister Splashy Pants."[25]

In the end, nearly 120,000 votes were cast for Mister Splashy Pants, collecting 78 percent of the ballot. The next highest name had 3 percent.[26]

The Internet community was ecstatic. Alexis Ohanian, cofounder of Reddit, explained it this way: "Everyone wants to hear their news anchor say, 'Mr. Splashy Pants.' That's what helped drive this."[27] Things turned out well for Greenpeace, too. They created a whole merchandising campaign around the name with shirts and pins that said, "Save Mister Splashy Pants." They also accomplished their mission. The free publicity and additional attention helped them convince the Japanese government to stop the whaling campaign.

What's the lesson here? When you launch something on the Internet, you have to be willing to lose control.[28] It no longer belongs exclusively to you. It becomes part of the wider community. And as Greenpeace discovered, that's OK.[29]

It's tempting for us in the Christian community to be uber serious about our mission. After all, it's not simply a matter of life or death. It's more important than that. We deal with spiritual realities and eternal destinies. But we can't control how people will respond to our message. The changing of human hearts is not human work. Perhaps if we loosened our grip and took ourselves a little less seriously, it would leave more room for God to work.

Faith sharing in any context is about relationship. We can fully engage with people in this brave new world of social media, and for the sake of Jesus's life-saving mission we should. But to be used by God to go global, we'll have to be willing to lose control.

Just like Jesus.

Prayer
    Lord Jesus, help me be willing to lose control for the sake of those in this world who don't know you yet.

Hiding God's Word in My Heart
    No one has greater love than to give up one's life for one's friends.

—Jesus, John 15:13 (CEB)

Discussion guide available at www.MeetTheGoodpeople.com.

Conclusion

Why Not Now?

When I pray, coincidences happen. When I don't, they don't.

—Archbishop William Temple

The best of all is, God is with us.

—John Wesley, shortly before he died at age eighty-seven

In the end, it all comes back to the Goodpeople. Across America, at least 180 million people are like our friends Joe and Sally—functionally non-Christian.[1] While Christianity is growing worldwide, adherents to the Christian faith in the United States are declining. Church attendance among younger generations is alarmingly low.[2] This little book proposes a spiritual revival. In many ways, spiritual conditions similar to ours existed in eighteenth-century England before the Holy Spirit ignited a renewal movement through John Wesley and others. The genius of the Wesleyan revival is found in the ways he engaged coldly indifferent people and turned them into warm-hearted disciples who changed the world. We can do that, too. We can recover the seven methods of the early Methodist movement that reached the nonchurched masses of that day. In short, they are:

Pray for God's heart for spiritually adrift people

Go to people where they are

82

Learn to speak their language

Tune in to their hearts in worship

Enfold awakened people in groups

Engage them in serving others

Go global with the message

If we will reshape these practices for a twenty-first century context and retool receptive individuals, groups, and churches to use them, a new wave of the Spirit will be released. We can be used by God in our time to lead vast numbers of pre-Christian people into a transforming relationship with Jesus and his church.

Jesus was crystal clear on his mission: "For the Son of Man came to seek and save those who are lost."[3] His first invitation to a couple of guys casting their nets was, "Come, follow me, and I'll show you how to fish for people."[4] Jesus is still angling for the people he loves, those that have drifted from his Father.

He's after good people like Jeff and Jenny. About seven years ago, these two showed up at church, liked it, and decided to go through our membership class. That's when I found out Jeff wasn't a believer. He liked Christianity. "If everyone lived like a Christian, we'd have world peace," he said. But he couldn't bring himself to commit. On the day his wife became a member, he stood by her side, but he couldn't say the vows.

Jenny soon became part of a moms' group led by my wife. Several women in the group had husbands who were not Christians, so they regularly prayed for their husbands, including Jeff, to come to Christ.

One spring, Jenny took a class on spiritual disciplines and was encouraged to attend a conference we were hosting at our church that August called The Global Leadership Summit. At first Jenny didn't think it was for her, but she decided to give it a try. Jenny was only able to attend part of the summit, but she was really inspired by one of the speakers, Bob Goff, the author of the widely popular book, *Love Does*. His effusive energy and down-to-earth message caught Jenny's heart: "Love God, love others, and do stuff!" Knowing her husband likes to take action, she thought Bob's message might just reach him. On that glimmer of hope, she bought the book.

Jeff is a busy guy with large responsibilities at work. That's in addition to their three active boys at home, so it took him a while to read the book. In November, he took it on a business trip to Houston. As he read on the plane, he could see why Jenny recommended it. It was both funny and meaningful. On his way home, he texted Jenny from Chicago to say how much he was enjoying the book. Even so, he knew she'd be disappointed. It was not the conversion experience she'd hoped it would be. A good book, for sure, but it just wasn't there.

Jeff boarded the commuter plane and kept reading. On the ground in Springfield, Jeff was leaving the plane when someone put a hand on his shoulder and said, "So, how do you like my book?"

Jeff said, "What do you mean?"

The man responded, "Hi, I'm Bob Goff."

In disbelief, Jeff replied, "Noooo, you're not Bob Goff." Jeff knew this national speaker and *New York Times* bestselling author lived in San Diego. He couldn't be on a little commuter plane touching down in Springfield, Illinois.

The man countered, "Yes, I am. Look!" He pointed to a guy in the terminal holding a sign. It said, "Bob Goff."

Jeff was speechless. For a moment, he could barely catch his breath. As they waited for their bags, the two of them had a chance to talk. He found out Bob was in town to speak at a youth conference. After rehearsing the whole story to the guy holding the sign, Jeff said, "Bob, I think you've just changed my life."

Bob said, "Let's get a picture." With knowing smiles, the two of them stood together next to the baggage claim. Jeff knew the number of details arranged for that moment could not be a coincidence. It blew the circuits of his rational mind and warmed his heart. For the first time in his life, he tasted a love beyond this world. "This is a sign," he said. "God is with me!"

A couple of weeks later, Jeff stood before our congregation and was baptized as a follower of Jesus Christ. The impact of his story has sent spiritual shock waves through his family, our church, and beyond. Jeff's now involved in a men's small group, a parenting class on Sunday morning, and figuring out where God's leading him to serve.

A few days after Jeff's airport experience, he said, "You know, deep down, I really wanted to believe. I just couldn't. I had no faith. I needed something that no one could arrange, a one-in-a-billion encounter."

"You needed something supernatural to happen," I suggested.

He reflected for a moment and said, "Yeah, I did."

Conclusion

God is still in the supernatural business. The movement of God's spirit is not confined to some distant place in a bygone era. "Jesus Christ is the same, yesterday, today, and forever!"[5] Deep down, most Christians I know want to be part of a world-changing movement where day by day the lost ones are found, the broken are healed, the separated are reconciled, and the poor are lifted up. But they feel trapped in ways of doing church that produce less and less fruit each year. Before you is an invitation to move forward by reaching back. Wesley and the early Methodist movement have much to offer us. If we'll humbly take their practices to heart, we too will experience a fresh movement of God.

Notes

Introduction

1. George G. Hunter III, *The Recovery of a Contagious Methodist Movement* (Nashville: Abingdon, 2011), 28.

2. Ed Stetzer, Richie Stanley, and Jason Hayes, *Lost and Found* (Nashville: B&H, 2009), 20–21.

3. Acts 2:47 NIV.

4. John Wesley, May 24, 1738, *Journals and Diaries I (1735–1738)*, ed. W. Reginald Ward and Richard P. Heitzenrater, vol. 18 of *The Bicentennial Edition of the Works of John Wesley* (Nashville: Abingdon, 1988), 250.

5. Ibid.

6. John Wesley, Letter to Jane Catherine March (March 29, 1760), *Letters III, 1756–1765*, ed. Ted A. Campbell, vol. 27 of *The Bicentennial Edition of the Works of John Wesley* (Nashville: Abingdon, forthcoming).

7. Mark 12:37 KJV.

8. John Wesley, Preface to Sermons on Several Occasions (1746), in *Sermons I: 1–33*, ed. Albert C. Outler, vol. 1 of *The Bicentennial Edition of the Works of John Wesley* (Nashville: Abingdon, 1984), 104.

1. Stay Close to the Power

1. World Methodist Council, "Member Churches," accessed May 29, 2015, http://worldmethodistcouncil.org/about/member-churches/.

2. Ezek 36:26 NIV.

3. Shared by Adam Hamilton during a main session of The Leadership Institute at The United Methodist Church of the Resurrection, Leawood, KS, September 27, 2013.

4. Kenda Creasy Dean, *Almost Christian: What the Faith of Our Teenagers Is Telling the American Church* (Oxford: Oxford University Press, 2010), 37.

5. King Duncan, ed., *King's Treasury of Dynamic Humor* (Knoxville, TN: Seven Worlds Corporation, 1990), 214.

6. Matt 7:7 NIV.

7. John 15:7.

8. Richard Foster, *Celebration of Discipline* (New York: Harper and Row, 1978), 30.

9. John Wesley, *Farther Thoughts upon Christian Perfection*, in *Doctrinal and Controversial Treatises II*, ed. Paul Wesley Chilcote and Kenneth J. Collins, vol. 13 of *The Bicentennial Edition of the Works of John Wesley* (Nashville: Abingdon, 2013), 127.

10. Jas 4:2 NIV.

11. John 15:5.

2. On the Go

1. Darren Rovell, "Super Bowl 2015: Tickets Priciest in History," ESPN, February 1, 2015, http://abcnews.go.com/Sports/sb-xlix-tickets-priciest-history/story?id=28646737.

2. Treacy Reynolds, "184 Million Americans to Watch 2015 Super Bowl, according to NRF Survey," National Retail Federation, January 22, 2015, https://nrf.com/media/press-releases/184-million-americans-watch-2015-super-bowl-according-nrf-survey; Prosper Insights and Analytics, *Monthly Consumer Survey* (January 2015), https://nrf.com/sites/default/files/Super%20Bowl%202015%20press_0.pdf.

3. "Super Snacking on Super Bowl," Fox News, January 31, 2015, http://www.foxnews.com/leisure/2012/01/31/super-snacking-on-super-bowl/.

4. "Super Bowl Statistics," Statistic Brain Research Institute, January 29, 2015, http://www.statisticbrain.com/super-bowl-statistics/.

5. "TV Viewership of the Super Bowl in the United States from 1990 to 2015 (in Millions)," Statista, accessed June 23, 2015, http://www.statista.com/statistics/216526/super-bowl-us-tv-viewership/; "Number of Views of the State of the Union Address

from 1993 to 2015 (in Millions)," Statista, accessed June 23, 2015, http://www.statista
.com/statistics/252425/state-of-the-union-address-viewer-numbers/.

6. Lindsay Kramer, "Super Bowl 2015: How Much Does a 30-Second Tele-vision Commercial Cost?" Syracuse.com, January 31, 2015, http://www.syracuse
.com/superbowl/index.ssf/2015/01/super_bowl_2015_how_much_does_commer
cial_cost_tv_ad_30_second_spot.html.

7. Greg Price, "Super Bowl 2014 Ratings: How Many Countries Will Watch the American Football Game?" *International Business Times*, January 30, 2014, http://www.ibtimes.com/super-bowl-2014-ratings-how-many-countries-will
-watch-american-football-game-1551791.

8. John 3:16.

9. John 3:17.

10. Richard P. Heitzenrater, *Wesley and the People Called Methodists*, 2nd. ed. (Nashville: Abingdon, 2013), 109.

11. John Wesley, March 29, 1739, *Journals and Diaries II (1738–43)*, ed. W. Reginald Ward and Richard P. Heitzenrater, vol. 19 of *The Bicentennial Edition of the Works of John Wesley* (Nashville: Abingdon, 1990), 46.

12. John Wesley, April 2, 1739, in Ward and Heitzenrater, *Journals and Diaries II*, 46.

13. Heitzenrater, *Wesley and the People Called Methodists*, 110.

14. Matt 28:19.

15. Craig Groeschel, presentation at Catalyst (presentation, Willow Creek Community Church, South Barrington, IL, November 8, 2012).

16. Lauren Leone-Cross, "Bible Study Meets Beer at 'Bar Church,'" *The State Journal-Register* (Springfield, IL), January 13, 2014, http://www.sj-r.com
/article/20140113/NEWS/140119727.

17. Ibid.

18. Jas 2:15-16 CEB.

19. Thom Rainer, *The Unchurched Next Door: Understanding Faith Stages as Keys to Sharing Your Faith* (Grand Rapids: Zondervan, 2003), 53.

20. Ibid., 64–76.

21. Matt 9:37 CEB.

22. Matt 9:38 CEB.

23. Luke 19:10 NLT.

24. Matt 4:19.

3. Plain Talk

1. Barna Group, *State of the Bible*, April 8, 2014, https://www.barna.org/barna-update/culture/664-the-state-of-the-bible-6-trends-for-2014#.VCCa7mePKpo.

2. Barna Group, "American Bible Society's State of the Bible 2014," http://www.americanbible.org/uploads/content/state-of-the-bible-2014-infographic-horizontal-american-bible-society.pdf.

3. Yasmin Anwar, "Americans and Religion Increasingly Parting Ways, New Survey Shows," UC Berkeley News Center, March 12, 2013, http://newscenter.berkeley.edu/2013/03/12/non-believers.

4. Sarah Eekhoff Zylstra, "Pew: Evangelicals Stay Strong as Christianity Crumbles in America," *Gleanings*, May 11, 2015, http://www.christianitytoday.com/gleanings/2015/may/pew-evangelicals-stay-strong-us-religious-landscape-study.html.

5. Anwar, "Americans and Religion Increasingly Parting Ways."

6. George Hunter, *How to Reach Secular People* (Nashville: Abingdon, 1992), 41.

7. Ian Burrell, "It's No Laughing Matter: Britain Has Become a Nation of Religious Illiterates 'Who Are Baffled by Biblical References in Monty Python Film *The Life of Brian*,'" *Independent*, October 18, 2013, http://www.independent.co.uk/news/media/tv-radio/its-no-laughing-matter-britain-has-become-a-nation-of-religious-illiterates-who-are-baffled-by-biblical-references-in-monty-python-film-the-life-of-brian-8890338.html.

8. "Scripture and Language Statistics 2014," Wycliffe Global Alliance, accessed June 23, 2015, http://www.wycliffe.net/resources/scriptureaccessstatistics/tabid/99/Default.aspx.

9. Rom 2:4 CEB.

10. Adam Hamilton, *Revival: Faith as Wesley Lived It* (Nashville: Abingdon, 2014), 113.

11. Gal 5:6.

12. Daniel M. Oppenheimer, "Consequences of Erudite Vernacular Utilized Irrespective of Necessity: Problems with Using Long Words Needlessly," *Applied Cognitive Psychology* 20 (2006): 153, doi:10.1002/acp.1178.

13. Mark 12:37 KJV.

14. John Wesley, Preface to Sermons on Several Occasions (1746), in *Sermons I: 1–33*, ed. Albert C. Outler, vol. 1 of *The Bicentennial Edition of the Works of John Wesley* (Nashville: Abingdon, 1984), 104.

15. John Bishop, "John Wesley: Plain Truth for Plain People," *Preaching*, May 1, 1987, http://www.preaching.com/resources/past-masters/11566916/.

16. John Wesley, Letter to the Rev. Samuel Furley (July 15, 1764), *Letters III (1756–1765)*, ed. Ted A. Campbell and Randy L. Maddox, vol. 27 of *The Bicentennial Edition of the Works of John Wesley* (Nashville: Abingdon, forthcoming).

17. George G. Hunter III, *The Recovery of a Contagious Methodist Movement* (Nashville: Abingdon, 2011), 19.

18. Ibid., 19–20.

4. Tune In to Their Hearts

1. Acts 2:47.

2. George G. Hunter III, *The Recovery of a Contagious Methodist Movement* (Nashville: Abingdon, 2011), 38.

3. Acts 10:44-45.

4. Hunter, *The Recovery of a Contagious Methodist Movement*, 38.

5. Acts 15:10-11.

6. David Packer, "The Cows Are in the Corn," *Night Time Thoughts* (blog), accessed July 7, 2015, http://nighttimethoughts.org/?p=1673. David Packer wrote the praise version of this joke. Graham Nickel claims to have written the hymn version in an April 15, 2012 (8:49 p.m.) comment on this blog post. Both versions are used with permission.

7. Ed Stetzer and Mike Dodson, *Comeback Churches* (Nashville: B&H, 2007), 65.

8. Richard P. Heitzenrater, *Wesley and the People Called Methodists*, 2nd ed. (Nashville: Abingdon, 2013), 259.

9. George Barna and David Kinnaman, eds., *Churchless: Understanding Today's Unchurched and How to Connect with Them* (Carol Stream, IL: Tyndale, 2014), 16–17.

10. Ibid., 12.

11. Matt 28:19.

12. Michael Paulson, "Megachurch with a Beat Lures a Young Flock," *New York Times*, September 9, 2014, http://www.nytimes.com/2014/09/10/us/hillsong -megachurch-with-a-beat-lures-a-young-flock.html?_r=1.

13. "Worship Options," North Coast Church, accessed June 24, 2015, http:// www.northcoastchurch.com/locations/vista-campus/worship-options/.

5. Do Life Together

1. Knowledge Networks and Insight Policy Research, *Loneliness among Old Adults: A National Survey of Adults 45+* (Washington, DC: AARP), http://assets .aarp.org/rgcenter/general/loneliness_2010.pdf.

2. Ethan Kross et al., "Facebook Use Predicts Declines in Subjective Well-Being in Young Adults," *PLoS ONE* 8, no. 8 (August 14, 2013), doi:10.1371/journal .pone.0069841.

3. Sherry Turkle, "The Flight from Conversation," *New York Times*, April 21, 2012, http://www.nytimes.com/2012/04/22/opinion/sunday/the-flight-from-con versation.html.

4. Gen 2:18.

5. John Ortberg, *Everybody's Normal Till You Get to Know Them* (Grand Rapids: Zondervan, 2003), 33.

6. John 10:38 CEB.

7. Ortberg, *Everybody's Normal*, 35.

8. Acts 2:42, 46-47 NIV.

9. Acts 20:20 CEB.

10. Jim Dethmer, "Strategies for Starting Churches" Seminar (lecture, Charles E. Fuller Institute, Pasadena, CA., February 18–19, 1991).

11. John Wesley, The 'Large' *Minutes*, A and B (1753, 1763), §4, in *The Methodist Societies: The Minutes of Conference*, ed. Henry D. Rack, vol. 10 of *The Bicentennial Edition of the Works of John Wesley* (Nashville: Abingdon, 2011), 845.

12. D. Michael Henderson, *John Wesley's Class Meeting: A Model for Making Disciples* (Nappanee, IN: Evangel, 1997), 18–19.

13. Ibid., 19.

14. Ibid., 20–21.

15. John Wesley, *The Nature, Design, and General Rules of the United Societies,* in *The Methodist Societies: History, Nature, and Design,* ed. Rupert E. Davies, vol. 9 of *The Bicentennial Edition of the Works of John Wesley* (Nashville: Abingdon, 1989), 69.

16. Ibid., 84.

17. Phil 2:13.

18. Henderson, *John Wesley's Class Meeting,* 93.

19. Heb 12:14.

20. Henderson, *John Wesley's Class Meeting,* 99.

21. "The Nature, Design, and General Rules of Our United Societies," in *The Book of Discipline of The United Methodist Church—2012,* ¶104 (Nashville: The United Methodist Publishing House, 2012), 76–78.

22. Henderson, *John Wesley's Class Meeting,* 107–8.

23. John Wesley, August 25, 1763, *Journals and Diaries IV (1755–65),* ed. W. Reginald Ward and Richard P. Heitzenrater, vol. 21 of *The Bicentennial Edition of the Works of John Wesley* (Nashville: Abingdon, 1992), 424.

24. "The Nature, Design, and General Rules of Our United Societies," in *The Book of Discipline, 2012,* ¶104, p. 76.

25. 2 Cor 5:17.

26. 1 Cor 8:1.

27. Gordon MacDonald, "My Small Group, Anonymous," *Leadership Journal* (Winter 2014): 32. © 2014 Christianity Today International. Used by permission of *Leadership Journal.* www.leadershipjournal.net.

6. Get Everyone in the Game

1. Paraphrased from Mark 10:42-44.

2. Mark 10:45 GNT.

3. Laurence J. Peter, as quoted at "Selfishness Quotes," Thinkexist.com, http://thinkexist.com/quotations/selfishness/.

4. Richard P. Fitzgibbons, "Selfishness in Youth," Child Healing: Strengthening Families, http://childhealing.com/articles/selfishchild.php.

5. Ibid.

6. W. Paul Jones, "Intentional Failure: The Importance of the Desert Experience," *Weavings* 7, no. 1 (January/February 1992), 20.

7. Eph 2:8-10.

8. Frank Viola and George Barna, *Pagan Christianity? Exploring the Roots of Our Church Practices* (Carol Stream, IL: Tyndale, 2008), 108.

9. 1 Pet 2:9 CEB.

10. John 15:16 CEB.

11. "Section III. Candidacy for Licensed and Ordained Ministry," in *The Book of Discipline of the United Methodist Church—2012*, ¶310 (Nashville: United Methodist Publishing House, 2012), 224.

12. D. Michael Henderson, *John Wesley's Class Meeting: A Model for Making Disciples* (Nappanee, IN: Evangel, 1997), 47.

13. Ibid., 48

14. Ibid., 50.

15. Rick Warren, *The Purpose Driven Life* (Grand Rapids: Zondervan, 2002), 17.

16. 1 Cor 12:4, 6-7 GNT.

17. There is no mutually agreed-upon list of spiritual gifts. In the New Testament, there are four key passages related to spiritual gifts: Rom 12:1-8; 1 Cor 12; Eph 4:4-16; 1 Pet 4:9-11.

18. "And serve each other according to the gift each person has received, as good managers of God's diverse gifts" (1 Pet 4:10 CEB).

19. "A demonstration of the Spirit is given to each person for the common good" (1 Cor 12:7 CEB).

20. "Christ is just like the human body—a body is a unit and has many parts. . . . You are the body of Christ and parts of each other" (1 Cor 12:12, 27 CEB).

21. Greg L. Hawkins and Cally Parkinson, *MOVE: What 1,000 Churches Reveal about Spiritual Growth* (Grand Rapids: Zondervan, 2011), 116.

22. Ibid.

7. Go Global

1. Richard P. Heitzenrater, *Wesley and the People Called Methodists*, 2nd ed. (Nashville: Abingdon, 2013), 110–11.

2. Ibid., 112.

3. Ibid.

4. "Twitter Accounts with the Most Followers Worldwide as of June 2015 (in Millions)," Statista: The Statistics Portal, accessed June 29, 2015, http://www.statista .com/statistics/273172/twitter-accounts-with-the-most-followers-worldwide/.

5. Vindu Goel, "Instagram Takes on Twitter with an Updated Photo Feed," *Times* Live, June 24, 2015, http://www.timeslive.co.za/scitech/2015/06/24/Insta gram-takes-on-Twitter-with-an-updated-photo-feed.

6. IANS, "Instagram Beats Twitter in Active Users," *New Indian Express*, December 20, 2014, http://www.newindianexpress.com/lifestyle/tech/Instagram -Beats-Twitter-in-Active-Users/2014/12/11/article2566254.ece.

7. "Number of Monthly Active Facebook Users Worldwide as of 1st Quarter 2015 (in Millions)," Statista: The Statistics Portal, accessed June 30, 2015, http:// www.statista.com/statistics/264810/number-of-monthly-active-facebook-users -worldwide/.

8. Lev Grossman, "Inside Facebook's Plan to Wire the World: Mark Zuckerberg's Crusade to Put Every Single Human Being Online," *TIME*, December 15, 2014, 32.

9. "Facebook Reports Third Quarter 2014 Results," Facebook Investor Relations, October 28, 2014, http://investor.fb.com/releasedetail.cfm?ReleaseID=878726.

10. "Facebook Statistics," Statistic Brain Research Institute, April 14, 2015, http://www.statisticbrain.com/facebook-statistics/.

11. Ted Coiné and Mark Babbitt, *A World Gone Social: How Companies Must Adapt to Survive* (New York: AMACOM, 2014), xv.

12. Leonard Sweet, *Viral: How Social Networking Is Poised to Ignite Revival* (Colorado Springs, CO: WaterBrook, 2012), 62.

13. Coiné and Babbitt, *World Gone Social*, xvi.

14. Ibid., 20.

15. Ibid.

16. Ibid.

17. Tim Nudd, "How a Fan Post on Panera's Facebook Page Got Half a Million Likes," Adweek, August 14, 2012, http://www.adweek.com/adfreak/how-fan-post -paneras-facebook-page-got-half-million-likes-142716.

18. Ibid.

19. Ibid.

20. Shared by Rick Warren in a teaching session at a Saddleback Church Leaders Conference in May 1995.

21. John 15:15 CEB.

22. Personal interview with Adam Hamilton on December 9, 2014.

23. Ibid.

24. "Mister Splashy Pants the Whale—You Named Him, Now Save Him," Greenpeace International, December 10, 2007, http://www.greenpeace.org/inter national/en/news/features/splashy-101207/.

25. Alexis Ohanian, "How to Make a Splash in Social Media" (TED talk, December, 2009), http://www.ted.com/speakers/alexis_ohanian.

26. "Mister Splashy Pants the Whale."

27. Ibid.

28. Ibid.

29. Laura McCormack, "Mr. Splashy Pants," *Second Chance Solutions* (blog), September 28, 2014, http://secondchancesolutions.blogspot.com/2014/09/mr -splashy-pants.html.

Conclusion

1. George G. Hunter III, *The Recovery of a Contagious Methodist Movement* (Nashville: Abingdon, 2011), 28.

2. George Barna and David Kinnaman, eds., *Churchless: Understanding Today's Unchurched and How to Connect with Them* (Carol Stream, IL: Tyndale, 2014).

3. Luke 19:10 NLT.

4. Matt 4:19 CEB.

5. Heb 13:8 CEB.

CPSIA information can be obtained
at www.ICGtesting.com
Printed in the USA
BVOW03s0504281216
471981BV00006B/158/P